The Philosopher's Tome

103 Ancient Greek and Roman Teachings for Contemporary Life

Raywat Deonandan

Intanjible Publishing

Dedicated to my father, who took seriously his rules for ethical and meaningful living; and to my mother, who knows intuitively to prioritize the finest virtues of love, compassion, forgiveness, and empathy.

Contents

How To Use This Book

"Books are the training weights of the mind." – Epictetus

I'VE BEEN TEACHING AT the university level for over 15 years now. In that time, I've noticed some alarming trends among the students who grace my classrooms. Many of my colleagues have noticed the same developments, as have friends who employ recent graduates. People in general, and young people in particular, are increasingly struggling to manage their emotions in response to the changing stressors of modern life.

Data back up this observation. A 2020 study published in the *Journal of Psychiatric Research* found a significant increase in anxiety among American adults from 2008 to 2018. The same study reported that the biggest increase was amongst those aged 18-25 years. There are probably many causes for this increase, which I won't enumerate here. But educators, families, and clinicians are trying many approaches to slow this concerning trend, with variable levels of success.

While the crushes of contemporary living appear to have had a lesser negative impact on us older folk, we are not totally immune. Personally, I have found myself retreating to the common-sense teachings of my late father to help get me through some challenging episodes. Timeless nuggets of cliched wisdom like, "Sticks and stones may break my bones but words will never hurt me" are proving invaluable in the cruel era of social media.

In recent years, I have found even more solace in the teachings of ancient masters of sagacity. The schools of Stoicism and Cynicism have proven particularly useful in helping me build resilience against an increasingly socially hostile and stressful online environment. I have in turn pointed some of my students to such timeless wisdom, and they have found it useful. A quick online search reveals that many other people, as well, are rediscovering classical philosophy as a means to calm their mounting mental distress.

Centuries ago, ancient philosophers refined and honed the cognitive tools that we so desperately need today. The knowledge and perspectives necessary to navigate an increasingly complicated and chaotic world have always been available to us. All that is required of us is to collate, study, and incorporate into our daily lives the lessons expounded by our wiser forebears.

For that reason, I have collected in this volume a curated menu of 103 quotes from 13 ancient Greek and Roman masters. These are the words that I have found useful in my own life, and that my students have in turn found useful for their own needs. It is my sincerest desire that you can put these words to use in your own life, as well.

You don't need any background in history or philosophy to read this book. All you need is a desire to bring some wisdom into your life. You may be surprised by how often certain themes are repeated by thinkers separated by centuries. Virtues like courage, gratitude, and compassion are repeated like a mantra chanted across generations, as are calls to eschew material gain in favour of spiritual growth and service to one's community. Clearly, some elements of personal fulfillment are indeed timeless.

Readers might wonder why some well-known quotes have been excluded, or why some philosophers are given more space than others. Why are Plato and Aristotle, who are indeed titans of the field, quoted only twice each, while Epictetus is quoted 30 times? The reason is that I have selected these quotes based on what I have found useful in my own life and in the lives of my students, and not based on their fame or familiarity. I clearly find Epictetus to be disproportionately an endless font of useful wisdom. That is my bias.

So, how should you read this book? You can start at the beginning and go right to the end; that is true. But the book is designed so that you can select a page at random, absorb its thought, then put the book aside until the next day, when you can select another page at random. Or if a particular philosopher appeals to you, you can consume their thoughts on a chapter-by-chapter basis. There are no rules.

Please note that in my personal life, I also regularly consult the teachings of ancient masters from other parts of the world. But this volume is deliberately dedicated to those who shaped Western thinking. If there is sufficient demand, future volumes will expound the wisdom of other cultures, as well.

Further, this book is written in Canadian English using Canadian spelling and grammar. I apologize if this frustrates my international readers!

Last, while I am a university professor, I am not an expert in philosophy or in ancient Greek or Roman history. What I offer is my own personal experience with these words, and the results of my own lengthy private study of their origins and intent, in hopes that they can best reach those who are ready to hear them. Those inspired to further their education in philosophy are encouraged to do so through other avenues, such as formal courses or dedicated books written by acknowledged scholars of the field.

Enjoy!

Raywat Deonandan, PhD

—

Reference:

Goodwin RD, Weinberger AH, Kim JH, Wu M, Galea S. Trends in anxiety among adults in the United States, 2008-2018: Rapid increases among young adults. *J Psychiatr Res.* 2020 Nov;130:441-446.

11 Quotes by Socrates

ANY BOOK PURPORTING TO explore the philosophers of ancient Greece and Rome must begin with Socrates. Born around 470 BC in Athens, he is considered one of the founders of Western philosophy and therefore one of the founders of Western civilization itself.

Socrates himself wrote nothing, or at least nothing that has survived. Our knowledge of his life and philosophy comes primarily through the accounts of his students, particularly Plato, as well as the playwright Aristophanes and the historian Xenophon.

Socrates is possibly best known for his method of inquiry, known as the Socratic Method, which involves asking probing questions to challenge assumptions and to stimulate critical thinking. This method is still widely used in education today.

His philosophy centered on ethics and the examination of the quality of human life, advocating for a focus on self-development over material wealth. He is thought to have said that "the unexamined life is not worth living," reflecting his belief in the importance of living a life that is deeply scrutinized and guided by virtue.

Socrates' disdain for sophistry and his relentless questioning of the Athens' political elite eventually led to his trial on charges of corrupting the youth and of impiety. He was sentenced to death by poison in 399 BC. His trial and death have been depicted as a seminal moment in classical philosophy and as a martyrdom for free speech and free thought.

The essence of his beliefs was that through relentless questioning and self-examination, one could achieve true knowledge, virtue, and "the good life".

Cropped from The Death of Socrates, oil painting by Jacques-Louis David in 1787

#1

"We cannot live better than in seeking to become better."
-Socrates

Socrates suggests that the highest form of living is not found in seeking external rewards or pleasures, but in the continuous effort to improve oneself morally, intellectually, and spiritually. This is a sentiment that is repeated somewhat in later schools of philosophical thought, including among Stoics and Cynics.

This philosophy aligns with Socrates' broader ethical teachings, which emphasize virtue and the development of one's character as the greatest goods. The pursuit of becoming a better person is, for Socrates, not only the most virtuous way to live but also the most fulfilling and meaningful. It involves a lifelong commitment to self-examination, learning, and the practice of virtues like wisdom, courage, and justice. Thus, according to Socrates, the best life is one dedicated to personal growth and ethical betterment.

Imagine a mid-level office worker in a stable but unfulfilling job. She decides to upgrade her skills by taking action and seeking additional training. In doing so, she improves her marketability and finds a more satisfying and upwardly mobile role. In the context of career development, actively seeking to become better through learning and skill enhancement not only improves personal competencies but also leads to professional opportunities and higher satisfaction.

The lesson is not limited to the workplace. Socrates would advise us to take the same approach to our relationships, our health, and our sense of greater belonging. Do not stagnate, but rather seek to be better, at all points in our lives.

A moment of contemplation.

#2

"Those who are hardest to love need it the most." -Socrates

Socrates believed that individuals who appear unlovable or difficult often behave this way because they lack love and acceptance in their lives. Their challenging behaviours might be defenses or reactions to deep-seated fears, insecurities, or past traumas.

Socrates suggests that instead of rejecting or avoiding difficult people, we should extend compassion and understanding toward them. Love and kindness can be transformative and healing. By offering love to those who seem to deserve it the least, we might help alleviate their suffering and potentially encourage positive changes in their behaviour.

This principle calls for patience, empathy, and a deep commitment to the well-being of others. It's a reminder of the power of compassion. This is a sentiment of great relevance to our modern times, when we are faced with a seemingly increasing number of people who anger us and challenge our sense of decorum. With disciplined intent, we can avoid the easy but unproductive path to anger and instead choose the far more constructive avenue of compassion.

Compassion and empathy

—ele—

#3

"Be kind, for everyone you meet is fighting a hard battle."
-Socrates

Although there is no direct historical source attributing this exact phrasing to Socrates, the sentiment is consistent with the empathetic characteristics of his philosophy.

The essence of this saying is that kindness is essential because every person one encounters is dealing with their own challenges, sorrows, or hardships, whether these are visible or hidden. This knowledge should foster compassion and understanding, prompting us to treat others with gentleness and patience, not anger.

The call for kindness is based on the recognition that since we can never fully know another's burdens, we should err on the side of empathy. This approach not only alleviates the hardships of others but also enriches our own moral character and contributes to a more humane and supportive society.

In our modern times of discord, highly prevalent mental illness, and short fuses, remembering this simple lesson can help us sustain a culture of calm tolerance instead of adding to the growing trend of hostility and strife.

Mutual support and understanding

#4

"The really important thing is not to live, but to live well. And to live well meant, along with more enjoyable things in life, to live according to your principles." -Socrates

This quote reflects Socrates's deep commitment to ethical living as the essence of a good life. In these words, he prioritizes not just existence but the quality and moral content of that existence.

For Socrates, to "live well" involves more than merely seeking pleasure or avoiding pain; it necessitates living in alignment with one's principles and virtues. This means actively engaging in self-reflection, cultivating virtues such as justice, courage, and wisdom, and making decisions based on these higher ethical standards rather than on whim or societal pressures.

The emphasis on "living according to your principles" suggests that true happiness and fulfillment come from a life that is congruent with one's deepest values and convictions. This not only guides one toward personal integrity but also enhances the well-being of the community. This idea remains a cornerstone of Socratic philosophy, promoting a life of thoughtful and principled action over mere survival.

Imagine an entrepreneur who starts a clothing business that prioritizes environmental sustainability over profit at all costs. She does so because supporting the environment aligns with her values. It also satisfies what she sees as being responsible to the needs of her community. Despite deprioritizing profit, her market differentiation attracts a loyal customer base who share her values, and her business becomes a modest success. The entrepreneur typifies the sentiment that true fulfillment comes from integrating one's values into daily actions and decisions, thereby achieving a meaningful and principled life.

The transfer of wisdom

#5

"Prefer knowledge to wealth, for the one is transitory, the other perpetual." -Socrates

Socrates believed in the lasting value of intellectual and moral development over material gains. By contrasting the transient nature of wealth with the enduring nature of knowledge, Socrates wishes us to consider the superiority of seeking wisdom, which he believed to be a permanent asset that enriches one's life in ways that material wealth cannot.

For Socrates, knowledge is not just a collection of facts but involves deep understanding and the ability to think critically and ethically. This kind of knowledge leads to a well-examined life, which Socrates famously regarded as the only life worth living. Unlike wealth, which can be lost or depleted and often leads to worry and conflict, knowledge fosters inner fulfillment, better decision-making, and a more profound connection to the world. His philosophy encourages prioritizing personal and intellectual growth, viewing it as the true path to lasting satisfaction and virtue.

The choice between enduring knowledge and ephemeral wealth.

#6

"To find yourself, think for yourself." -Socrates

According to Socrates, true understanding of oneself cannot be attained by merely adopting the opinions and beliefs of others. Instead, it requires active, critical thinking and introspection.

This idea is central to Socratic philosophy, which emphasizes the role of questioning and dialogue in uncovering deeper truths. By encouraging individuals to think for themselves, Socrates advocates for a life of intellectual autonomy in which we examine our own beliefs, values, and motivations. This process of self-reflection and critical inquiry leads to genuine self-discovery and a more authentic, meaningful life. Essentially, Socrates is championing the idea that personal identity and wisdom are forged through the diligent exercise of reason and judgement, rather than through passive acceptance of external influences.

The pursuit of personal understanding.

#7

"An unexamined life is not worth living." -Socrates

This is one of Socrates's most famous statements. For him, the essence of a meaningful and fulfilling life lies in continuously questioning and examining one's beliefs, values, and actions. This process of self-examination leads to greater self-awareness, moral integrity, and personal growth.

Socrates held that without examining our lives, we risk living superficially, adhering to unchallenged assumptions and societal norms without understanding their true nature or implications. This lack of reflection can lead to a life devoid of purpose and authenticity. An examined life, however, involves seeking wisdom, understanding the reasons behind our actions, and striving to live virtuously.

In this quote, Socrates is advocating for a life of active engagement with our own minds and values. He believed that through this continuous process of self-examination, we can achieve true knowledge, make ethical choices, and live a life of deeper significance and fulfillment. Thus, an unexamined life, lacking in such critical introspection, fails to reach its full potential and is not truly worth living.

The beginning of self-examination.

#8

"Beware the barrenness of a busy life." -Socrates

In this quote, Socrates is concerned that being excessively busy, often with trivial or unimportant tasks, can lead to a life lacking in meaningful substance and fulfillment. A life consumed by ceaseless activity, without reflection or purpose, can be ultimately unfruitful and empty.

Socrates is encouraging us to make time for introspection and to prioritize activities that genuinely enrich our lives and align with our values, rather than merely filling our time with activities. It's a reminder of the value of pausing, reflecting, and ensuring that our actions are purposeful and contribute to a fulfilling life.

The sterility and emptiness of an overly busy life.

#9

"My friend...care for your psyche...know thyself, for once we know ourselves, we may learn how to care for ourselves."
-Socrates

Socrates taught that understanding oneself is the foundation of personal growth and ethical living. The term "psyche" here is not just about mental or emotional health, but encompasses the entirety of moral and rational essence.

The phrase "know thyself," famously associated with Socrates and inscribed at the Temple of Apollo at Delphi, is a timeless call to understand our true nature, motivations, and desires. This deep self-knowledge is pivotal because it determines how we should live and act. By fully grasping our strengths, weaknesses, and intrinsic motivations, we are better equipped to make choices that not only enhance our well-being but also align with virtuous living.

Such self-awareness ensures we care for ourselves in a comprehensive manner, fostering not only physical well-being but also nurturing our moral and intellectual growth.

The journey of self-knowledge and self-care.

#10

"Let him who would move the world first move himself."
-Socrates

Socrates suggests that anyone who aspires to create meaningful change in the world must first focus on transforming oneself. This means that before attempting to influence or reform others, one should work on one's own character, knowledge, and behaviour. Personal integrity and self-awareness are crucial, as they form the foundation for effective leadership and influence. By improving oneself, a person becomes more capable, credible, and ethical, thereby setting a positive example for others to follow.

Furthermore, Socrates argues that true change begins from within. When we strive to better ourselves, we develop the wisdom, empathy, and strength needed to address larger societal issues. This inward journey of self-improvement not only enhances personal capabilities but also inspires and empowers others to do the same. Socrates' quote underscores the interconnectedness of personal and societal transformation, advocating for a focus on self-discipline and self-awareness as the first steps towards moving and changing the world.

The challenge of personal change.

#11

"True wisdom comes to each of us when we realize how little we understand about life, ourselves, and the world around us." -Socrates

Socrates suggests that genuine wisdom begins with the acknowledgment of our own limitations and ignorance. Many people believe they have a comprehensive understanding of life, themselves, and the world, but Socrates argues that this sense of certainty is often misguided. By admitting how little we truly know, we open ourselves up to continual learning and growth. This humility is crucial because it prevents complacency and encourages a lifelong pursuit of knowledge and self-improvement. For Socrates, the wisest individuals are those who recognize the vastness of what they do not know and remain curious and open-minded.

Furthermore, Socrates' quote highlights the philosophical stance that wisdom is not about having all the answers, but about asking the right questions and being aware of the complexity and mystery of existence. This perspective fosters a sense of wonder and inquisitiveness, motivating individuals to seek deeper understanding and truth. By realizing our own ignorance, we become more receptive to new ideas, experiences, and perspectives, which can lead to greater insight and enlightenment. In essence, Socrates is advocating for a humble and inquisitive approach to life, where true wisdom is found in the continuous quest for understanding rather than in the possession of absolute knowledge.

Realizing one's own smallness and the pursuit of true wisdom.

2 Quotes by Plato

PLATO WAS ONE OF the most influential philosophers in Western history, born around 428 BC in Athens. A student of Socrates and the teacher of Aristotle, Plato laid much of the foundational structures for Western philosophy and science. He founded the Academy, one of the earliest known organized schools in Western history, where he taught until his death around 347 BC.

His work covers a vast array of subjects including ethics, politics, metaphysics, epistemology, and the philosophy of language. His dialogues, where characters discuss philosophical issues through conversational exchanges, have been used to explore these topics. The most famous of these dialogues is perhaps "The Republic," which outlines a vision of a just society.

Plato's influence cannot be overstated. His ideas shaped Western thought on government, ethics, and philosophy. The Academy persisted as a center of learning until AD 529, when it was closed by Byzantine emperor Justinian I who opposed its pagan origins. Yet Plato's work laid the groundwork for the emergence of Christian theology and the development of much of Western philosophical tradition.

It's difficult to summarize Plato's beliefs in a single sentence. But in short, he believed in the existence of immutable, perfect forms that represent the true essence of all things in the material world... which he argued is only a shadow of the real, ideal world that is best accessed through reason and philosophical inquiry.

*Plato, copy of the portrait made by Silanion ca. 370 BC
for the Academia in Athens*

#1

"The worst of all deceptions is self-deception." -Plato

Self-deception involves convincing oneself of a version of reality that is either more comfortable or preferable than the truth. This can lead to a distorted view of oneself, one's abilities, and the world, which ultimately undermines personal growth and moral integrity. For Plato, knowing oneself is fundamental to philosophy and to the pursuit of virtue.

But what does it mean to "know oneself"? Plato would argue that it has something to do with achieving an honest understanding of one's true nature, strengths and limitations.

Imagine a manager who received a formal performance review that states he is too authoritarian and unempathetic. But instead of deeply considering the implications of the review, the manager instead chooses to believe his behaviour is firm and "results driven", discounting the opinions of others. The result is that he will probably be denied opportunities for personal and professional growth, much to his own detriment and that of his organization. Ignoring or rationalizing away valid criticisms can have serious consequences for oneself and one's social network.

Plato was a believer in the supreme importance of introspection and a commitment to the truth, especially to oneself. In short, when we are not truthful with ourselves, we are less likely to acknowledge our flaws, mistakes, and areas for improvement. This can result in a stagnant and unfulfilled life, as we are unable to address the root causes of our problems.

Beware the image you see before you.

——⁓ℓℓ⁓——

#2

"We can easily forgive a child who is afraid of the dark; the real tragedy of life is when men are afraid of the light." -Plato

There is some controversy about whether this is in fact attributable to Plato. But the sentiment does align with the body of his teachings. In this quote, Plato acknowledges that it's natural for children to fear what they do not understand or cannot see. This fear is seen as forgivable because it stems from a straightforward, undeveloped understanding of the world.

But it is tragic when adults, who are capable of rational thought and enlightenment, nevertheless fear truth or knowledge. Both Plato and his teacher Socrates viewed the deliberate avoidance of understanding or enlightenment as a fundamental failure of human potential. They believed that the pursuit of knowledge and truth was essential for a worthwhile life. It is a profound misfortune when adults resist enlightenment, preferring the comfort of ignorance over the challenges and responsibilities that come with knowledge. The seeking of truth is a path to virtuous and fulfilling living.

Consider someone who avoids medical check-ups or ignore symptoms due to fear of receiving bad news or having to confront a serious health issue. Their avoidance of the "light" of medical knowledge can lead to worsened health outcomes that could have been preventable with earlier intervention.

Innocent fear of the dark vs apprehension towards the light.

2 Quotes by Aristotle

ARISTOTLE, BORN IN 384 BC in Stagira, a small town on the northern coast of Greece, was a towering figure in ancient philosophy, making profound contributions to logic, metaphysics, mathematics, physics, biology, botany, ethics, politics, agriculture, medicine, dance, and theatre. He is often regarded as one of the three most influential philosophers in Western thought, alongside Plato and Socrates.

Aristotle's father was the personal physician to King Amyntas of Macedon, which likely influenced Aristotle's later interest in the natural sciences. At the age of seventeen or eighteen, he moved to Athens to join Plato's Academy, where he remained for about twenty years, first as a student and later as a teacher.

After Plato's death, Aristotle served as a tutor to Alexander the Great. And when Alexander began his legendary conquests, Aristotle returned to Athens and established his own school, the Lyceum. Unlike Plato's Academy, the Lyceum had a strong emphasis on empirical research.

Aristotle wrote extensively, though much of his writings have been lost. His surviving works have been incredibly influential and cover a wide range of topics, including logic, ethics, politics, and the natural sciences.

Aristotle's methods and ideas formed an integral part of Islamic and Medieval scholastic philosophy. His influence extended well into the Renaissance and continues to be integral to philosophical and scientific discourse today. His work forms a cornerstone of the Western philosophical tradition, affecting a broad spectrum of knowledge.

In essence, Aristotle believed in the pursuit of knowledge as a method to understand the natural world and achieve a good life

Bust of Aristotle. Roman copy after a
Greek bronze original by Lysippos from
330 BC

\#1

"You will never do anything in this world without courage. It is the greatest quality of the mind next to honour." -Aristotle

In Aristotle's ethical framework, courage is not merely physical bravery, but also moral courage. Courage is exercising the strength to uphold principles, make difficult decisions, and to act with integrity even in the face of adversity. By stating that courage is the greatest quality of the mind next to honour, Aristotle places it at the core of virtuous living.

Honour, which encompasses qualities like integrity, fairness, and respect, is also a central virtue in Aristotle's overall philosophy. Together, courage and honour form the bedrock of a virtuous character, enabling us to pursue excellence ("arete") and to lead fulfilling lives.

Aristotle teaches that without courage, we cannot consistently act according to our values or achieve greatness. Courage is what empowers us to live honourably and to realize our potential, making it an indispensable quality for any significant accomplishment or virtuous life.

Overcoming personal challenges such as battling a severe illness or recovering from a major setback, like losing a loved one, requires personal courage. We must face our situations, make tough decisions, and continue moving forward despite pain and uncertainty.

Readiness to face the unknown.

#2

"We are what we repeatedly do. Excellence, then, is not an act, but a habit." -Aristotle

This quote is actually a rephrasing by historian Will Durant of a much longer Aristotelian statement. In it, Aristotle suggests that our identity and character are shaped by our consistent actions and behaviours. What we do regularly forms our habits, and these habits define who we are. Excellence, therefore, is not achieved through a single act or a momentary effort but through the repeated and consistent practice of good habits. This means that to become excellent or to achieve greatness in any field, one must engage in regular and disciplined practice. It's the accumulation of these small, consistent actions over time that leads to excellence.

Aristotle is arguing that excellence is a result of deliberate and intentional effort. It is not an innate quality or a one-time achievement, but a continuous process of improvement and refinement. By focusing on developing good habits and practicing them consistently, we can cultivate excellence in various aspects of our lives. Aristotle encourages us to prioritize consistent effort and perseverance, recognizing that true excellence comes from sustained commitment and hard work.

Consider a marathon runner. Her excellence is not achieved through occasional practice but through daily rigorous training routines, proper nutrition, and regular races. The consistency in training develops the stamina, skill, and mental toughness required to excel.

Excellence emerges from repetition.

8 Quotes by Epicurus

E picurus was an ancient Greek philosopher born in 341 BC on the island of Samos. He founded a school of philosophy in Athens, which was known as the Garden. His philosophy, Epicureanism, became one of the major philosophical systems of the Hellenistic period (those years between the death of Alexander the Great in 323 BC and the rise of Roman domination in 31 BC.) Epicureanism had a significant influence on later thought, including during the European Renaissance.

Epicurus's philosophy centered on the pursuit of happiness, which he believed could be achieved through the attainment of pleasure and the avoidance of pain. However, his view of pleasure was sophisticated and not just a form of hedonism. Pleasure was to be found in the absence of pain, a tranquil state of mine (which he called "ataraxia"), simple living, and friendship.

Importantly, Epicurus argued that unnecessary fears, especially fear of the gods and death, are obstacles to happiness. He believed that gods exist; but he thought that the gods were not concerned with human affairs. Death, he argued, is the cessation of sensation and should not be feared, as we do not exist either to experience pain or pleasure after it.

Today, Epicurean philosophy is recognized for its contributions to the development of science and ethics. Epicurus's letters and maxims continue to be studied for their insights into achieving a contented life.

In essence, Epicurus believed that the greatest good is to seek modest pleasures in order to attain a state of tranquility and freedom from fear, along with the absence of bodily pain, through knowledge, friendship, and living a virtuous and wise life.

Epicurus, Roman copy after a lost Hellenistic original.

#1

"The noble man is chiefly concerned with wisdom and friendship; of these, the former is a mortal good, the latter an immortal one." -Epicurus

Epicurus wished to inspire us to hold wisdom and friendship as core values in our lives. This statement suggests that wisdom helps us navigate our mortal journey effectively, while friendship creates an immortal legacy of bonding and affection. By valuing both wisdom and friendship, we can aim to live virtuous lives that make a significant and enduring difference in the world, during our lifetimes and beyond.

Relationships we build in our networks through collegiality and friendships can outlive our mortal bodies in that they formed their scaffolding of community, upon which the relationships of future generations are built.

Epicurus is advocating for a balanced focus on personal development through wisdom and the nurturing of enduring relationships through friendship, both of which are essential for a noble and fulfilling life.

Wisdom and friendship.

#2

"He who has peace of mind disturbs neither himself nor another." -Epicurus

With this statement, Epicurus is emphasizing the profound impact of inner tranquility on one's interactions and relationships. According to Epicurean philosophy, achieving peace of mind (ataraxia) is essential for living a fulfilled and happy life. This inner peace is characterized by the absence of distress and emotional turmoil.

Epicurus taught that when an individual attains such a state, he is not only content within himself but also incapable of causing disturbance or harm to others. This is because inner tranquility aligns with rational thinking and the avoidance of unnecessary desires that typically lead to conflict and suffering. (To the modern mind, this sounds almost Buddhist). The peace of mind ensures that one acts considerately and harmoniously, promoting both personal well-being and positive relations with others.

Thus, for Epicurus, cultivating a peaceful and serene mind is crucial not just for personal happiness but also for maintaining social harmony and goodwill.

The tranquility of a peaceful mind that does not disturb itself or others.

\#3

"Do not spoil what you have by desiring what you have not. Remember that what you now have was once among the things you only hoped for." -Epicurus

This quote conveys a key principle of Epicurus' philosophical outlook, which emphasizes contentment and the avoidance of unnecessary desires. These two simple sentences offer at least four lessons:

First, we must not allow our desires for things we don't have diminish our appreciation for what we currently possess. Epicurus suggests that excessive desire for more can lead to dissatisfaction and unrest, which are contrary to a peaceful life.

Second, Epicurus advocates for mindfulness about the transient nature of desire. He reminds us that many things we currently have were once just desires. This reflection is meant to foster gratitude and a deeper appreciation for what one already possesses, recognizing that past desires have been fulfilled.

Third, true happiness comes from simple pleasures and the absence of pain (what Epicurus called "aponia") and disturbance ("ataraxia"). By curbing unnecessary desires—especially those for wealth, power, and fame—perhaps we can maintain a tranquil state of mind. Epicurus believed that the key to happiness was to desire less rather than to acquire more.

Fourth, the quote speak to an overall philosophical contentment, which to the Epicureans meant living a self-sufficient life surrounded by friends, and finding joy in simple pleasures. In this way, we avoid the anxieties and disturbances that come with pursuing insatiable desires.

The quote is essentially about finding happiness in the present and learning to be satisfied with what we have, rather than being caught in an endless cycle of desire and dissatisfaction.

Satisfaction.

\#4

"He who is not satisfied with a little is satisfied with nothing."
-Epicurus

Contentment does not come from the amount of possessions or wealth one has, but from one's attitude towards them. While Epicurus was not a Stoic, this statement does reflect a core Stoic belief in the importance of moderation and self-sufficiency.

The principle behind this saying is that if a person cannot find happiness in having a small amount, increasing that amount is unlikely to bring satisfaction either. Such a person is always in pursuit of more, driven by insatiable desires that can never be fully met, resulting in a perpetual state of dissatisfaction and discontent.

Epicurean philosophy values simple living and the pursuit of mental tranquility over the accumulation of wealth or luxury. Epicurus taught that true happiness comes from within and is achieved through the cultivation of a tranquil mind, free from unnecessary desires and fears.

Fulfillment in simplicity.

#5

"Death is nothing to us. When we exist, death is not; and when death exists, we are not. All sensation and consciousness end with death and therefore in death there is neither pleasure nor pain. The fear of death arises from the belief that in death, there is awareness." -Epicurus

The fear of death is irrational because death itself involves the absence of sensation and consciousness, conditions necessary for experiencing fear or any emotion. For Epicurus, life is about the pursuit of pleasure and the avoidance of pain, a philosophy known as Hedonism. Since death is devoid of both sensation and consciousness, it neither contains pleasure nor pain, and thus should not be a source of fear.

Epicurus argues that while we are alive, death is not present, and once we die, we no longer exist to experience anything, including death itself. Therefore, worrying about death is pointless and detracts from enjoying life. This perspective is intended to liberate individuals from the fear of death, encouraging them to focus on living a fulfilling life based on the pleasures of the present without the anxiety over an inconsequential end.

Neither sensation nor consciousness.

#6

"The art of living well and the art of dying well are one."
-Epicurus

Epicurus often explored the interconnections between life and death for the purpose of achieving peace and contentment. This quote reflects this holistic view, emphasizing that the principles guiding a well-lived life also help prepare for a peaceful death.

For Epicurus, living well involves cultivating virtues, enjoying simple pleasures, and minimizing pain and fear, particularly the fear of death. He believed that by understanding the natural process of death and accepting it as a part of life, we could live free of the anxiety that often accompanies thoughts of mortality. This acceptance enables us to focus on living a fulfilling and ethical life, characterized by tranquility and happiness.

In this view, if one lives well, embracing a philosophy that promotes mental peace and contentment, then dying well—without fear and at peace—naturally follows. This philosophy underscores the inseparability of life and death in the pursuit of a well-rounded and contented existence.

Life and death are a continuous, harmonious flow.

#7

"It is folly for a man to pray to the gods for that which he has the power to obtain by himself." -Epicurus

Epicurus believed that many of the things people seek through prayer or divine intervention are within their own capacity to achieve through effort, reason, and action.

This idea encourages us to take responsibility for our own lives and well-being rather than relying on external forces or deities. By emphasizing individual agency, Epicurus promotes a proactive approach to life. He suggests that it is more sensible and effective to use our own abilities and resources to solve problems and to achieve goals rather than passively hoping for divine intervention. This perspective aligns with his broader philosophy, which values self-sufficiency, personal effort, and the pursuit of a rational, fulfilling life.

Self-reliance obviates the need for divine intervention.

#8

"You don't develop courage by being happy in your relationships every day. You develop it by surviving difficult times and challenging adversity." -Epicurus

This statement teaches that courage isn't cultivated during easy or comfortable times, but rather through facing and overcoming hardships. It suggests that true strength of character is built through enduring challenges, not when circumstances are favourable. Such experiences force us to confront our fears, push beyond our comfort zones, and develop resilience.

While this idea is somewhat universal and could resonate with various philosophical teachings, it is more typically associated with philosophies that focus explicitly on virtue ethics and the development of character through adversity, such as Stoicism. Epicureanism, in contrast, generally advocates for the avoidance of pain and the pursuit of pleasure in a measured way, emphasizing tranquility as the path to happiness. In short, Epicureanism focuses on the pursuit of happiness through moderating desires and cultivating friendships.

Resilience and courage through adversity.

2 Quotes by Heraclitus

Heraclitus was an ancient Greek philosopher from Ephesus, part of the Persian Empire around 535–475 BC. He is sometimes referred to as the "weeping philosopher" for his melancholic tone of his surviving thoughts, or as the "obscure philosopher" due to the enigmatic nature of his writings.

Some modern observers see many parallels between the positions of Heraclitus and the Buddha. Interestingly, the 19th century philosopher Hegel felt that Heraclitus was the first true philosopher in human history for recognizing that opposites, such as good and bad, change over time as society changes perspective.

Heraclitus posited that the universe is characterized by a constant struggle of opposites and that this tension is actually necessary for life. He believed that conflict is a fundamental aspect of existence. His most famous assertion, "You cannot step into the same river twice," captures his belief that everything is in constant flux and that stability is an illusion. This idea of perpetual change as a fundamental characteristic of the universe was revolutionary at the time, and forms a central part of his philosophy.

Heraclitus also introduced the concept of the "Logos", a fundamental order or reason that governs the cosmos. Although interpretations vary, one view is that Logos is an underlying principle of reality that explains the consistent and predictable patterns of change in the universe. Heraclitus suggested that while most people live as if they are asleep, the wise recognize and align themselves with this Logos.

His ideas significantly influenced later philosophical traditions, including Stoicism –a major part of this collection-- which incorporated his emphasis on the underlying order and reason in nature. His work also resonates with modern philosophical movements that emphasize embracing change.

Despite his profound influence, only fragments of Heraclitus's writings survive, often quoted by later philosophers. His thought challenges readers to recognize the constancy of change and the complexity of the world, urging a deeper engagement with the mysteries of the universe.

Heraclitus

#1

"There is nothing permanent except change." -Heraclitus

Everything is in a constant state of flux. Stability or permanence is merely an illusion. According to Heraclitus, life and the world are continuously transforming, and this ceaseless change is the only constant we can rely on. By emphasizing change as the only permanent thing, Heraclitus highlights the importance of embracing transformation and understanding that our experiences and realities are always evolving. This perspective challenges us to remain adaptable and open to the continuous flow of life.

Change is the only constant.

\#2

"Big results require big ambitions." -Heraclitus

Through this aphorism, Heraclitus suggests that significant achievements are not a product of circumstance or incremental effort. Rather, they require substantial, ambitious goals.

This is a call to set our sights high, as the scale of our ambitions directly influences the magnitude of our potential achievements. This idea not only encourages striving for lofty goals but also underlines a fundamental principle of cause and effect: that great endeavors are necessary precursors to great results.

In a broader philosophical context, Heraclitus is commenting on the importance of having the courage and vision to pursue challenging and grand objectives, thereby driving transformative changes and outcomes. So many of us harbour a desire for dramatic positive changes in our lives, but lack the pluck, tenacity, and vision to set ourselves on the path to achieve those changes. Heraclitus calls on us to find that mettle.

The scale of ambition required to achieve significant results.

7 Quotes by Plutarch

Though Greek, Plutarch was born around 46 AD in the small town of Chaeronea, in the Roman province of Boeotia. He lived during the early Imperial period of Rome, enjoying a long life that lasted until about 120 AD. Plutarch's extensive writings, particularly his parallel biographies of prominent Greeks and Romans, have made him one of the most influential ancient historians.

While more of a biographer and essayist than a philosopher in the classical sense, his explorations of the lives and perspectives of prominent contemporaries saw uncommon wisdom flow from Plutarch's pen. His most famous work is "Parallel Lives," a series of biographies of famous Greek and Roman men, presented in tandem to illuminate their common moral virtues and failings. This work provides valuable insights into Greek and Roman culture and has been immensely influential in shaping the historical perception of figures such as Alexander the Great and Julius Caesar.

In addition, Plutarch wrote a collection of essays that cover a vast array of subjects, including ethics, religion, philosophy, and education. While he was known as a follower of Plato, he also incorporated elements from other philosophical schools, such as Stoicism, into his writings. His philosophy often focused on ethics, practical wisdom, and the moral issues involved in political leadership. He was interested in the moral character of those he profiled, and what modern readers could learn from such conduct.

Plutarch's works were a significant source of inspiration during the Renaissance and helped shape the moral ideals of European and American intellectual life. His biographies have been read as moral guides and were particularly revered by Shakespeare.

Bust of Plutarch at the Delphi Archaeological Museum

#1

"An imbalance between rich and poor is the oldest and most fatal ailment of all republics." -Plutarch

Economic inequality is not a new problem but a longstanding one that has threatened the viability of republics throughout history. When wealth is concentrated in the hands of a few, it can lead to a concentration of power and influence that marginalizes the majority, fostering resentment, disenfranchisement, and potentially leading to social upheaval.

Plutarch's insight is a warning that for a republic to thrive, it must address and manage economic disparities among its citizens effectively.

Rich and poor.

\#2

"The mind is not a vessel to be filled, but a fire to be kindled." -Plutarch

This perspective shifts the focus of education from merely transferring knowledge—as if pouring water into an empty jug—to inspiring and stimulating the mind. Teaching should be about encouraging curiosity, critical thinking, and a passion for inquiry. In this contraction from the lengthier original statement, Plutarch suggests that true education should awaken a student's intellectual capabilities and cultivate a lifelong enthusiasm for learning and discovery.

In essence, Plutarch is advocating for an approach to education that is transformative rather than transactional. It should not only inform but also inspire, not merely depositing facts but fostering the ability to think independently, question, and explore.

The flames of learning.

#3

"Do not speak of your happiness to one less fortunate than yourself." -Plutarch

One should strive for empathy and discretion in social interactions. This advice is rooted in the principle of respect for the emotional states of individuals who may be experiencing hardship or suffering.

By advising against discussing one's own happiness with those who are less fortunate, Plutarch is highlighting the importance of being considerate and mindful of the potential for envy or sorrow that such conversations might provoke. Discussing one's good fortune in the presence of someone who is struggling can be seen as insensitive or tactless. It may, in fact, inadvertently heighten their sense of deprivation or unhappiness.

This guidance encourages a thoughtful and compassionate approach to communication, urging individuals to tailor their interactions based on the circumstances and feelings of those around them. It underscores the value of kindness and the need to foster positive, supportive relationships rather than exacerbating feelings of inequality or misfortune.

The affluent and the distressed.

#4

"Music, to create harmony, must investigate discord."
-Plutarch

In music, harmony is achieved when different notes or chords sound pleasing together, but this pleasing effect is often enhanced by the resolution of discordant or dissonant elements. The presence of discord creates a sense of tension or conflict that, when resolved, makes the harmonious parts more impactful and satisfying.

Metaphorically, Plutarch's statement can be applied to life and human experience. To achieve true harmony and balance in life, one must confront and understand the challenges, conflicts, and difficulties— the "discords"—that arise. By addressing and resolving these issues, a deeper and more meaningful harmony can be achieved. Plutarch is stressing the importance of embracing and investigating discord as a necessary step toward creating harmony, whether in art, personal growth, or societal relations.

Harmony and discord.

#5

"It is certainly desirable to be well descended, but the glory belongs to our ancestors." -Plutarch

Plutarch acknowledges that while it is beneficial and often advantageous to come from a distinguished or noble lineage, the true honour and achievements associated with that lineage belong to the ancestors themselves, not to their descendants.

The essence of his message is that we should not rely solely on our heritage or family background for our sense of worth or accomplishment. Instead, we are encouraged to create our own legacies and earn respect through personal virtues, achievements, and contributions. This viewpoint promotes the idea that we are all responsible for our own actions and should strive to attain our own glory through personal effort and integrity, rather than resting on the laurels of our forebears.

The relevance to modern life is fairly obvious. We see "legacies" everywhere, even in ostensible meritocracies. Mediocre students are afforded entry into top schools because of family lineage, not high grades. Scions of past elected leaders suddenly find themselves in political leadership positions due to their surnames and not to any extraordinary political skills. The so-called "nepo baby" trend of many Hollywood stars being children of Hollywood stars is now regularly called out in social media. These achievements are shallow, unfair, and do not lead to fulfillment or personal growth.

Individual glory must be earned, not merely inherited.

#6

"Painting is silent poetry." -Plutarch

In Plutarch's profound view, both the visual art of painting and the literary art of poetry can convey deep emotions, complex ideas, and universal truths without direct verbal communication. Both forms of art, despite their different mediums, achieve similar ends. They both evoke feelings, tell stories, and express aspects of the human experience through symbolic representation.

Paintings, like poems, communicate through a language of their own: one made of shapes, colours, forms, and compositions. These elements are analogous to the words, rhythms, and structures used in poetry, and allow painters to articulate thoughts and stir emotions subtly and powerfully, much as poets do through verse.

Plutarch is reminding us of the evocative power of art and its capacity to speak directly to the soul. We all need some form of art in our lives, both in consumption and creation. In our modern leaves, we are daily assaulted by other people's creative visions, in the form of television shows, movies, books, and even ubiquitous advertising. But those who take the time to express themselves artistically, at whatever level of creativity they can summon, can reap considerable rewards in terms of calmness, resilience, and empathy.

Scenes can be as lyrical as words.

#7

"Know how to listen, and you will profit even from those who talk badly." -Plutarch

Plutarch suggests that the skill of listening is valuable in its own right, independent of the quality of the speaker's delivery. By truly listening and paying attention, one can extract useful information, insights, or lessons even from those who might not express themselves well. This requires patience, discernment, and the ability to look beyond superficial flaws in communication. Effective listening involves focusing on the content of the message rather than being distracted by the speaker's style or errors. In doing so, a listener can find value in almost any conversation, learning something new or gaining a different perspective.

Furthermore, Plutarch's quote underscores the broader principle that wisdom and learning opportunities can come from unexpected sources. By being open-minded and attentive, individuals can gain knowledge and understanding from a wide range of experiences and interactions. This approach aligns with the idea that everyone has something to offer, and that there is always something to be learned, even in imperfect circumstances. It encourages humility and a willingness to find merit in diverse voices, fostering a mindset that values continuous learning and personal growth. In essence, Plutarch is advocating for the cultivation of listening as a means to gain wisdom and benefit from all interactions, regardless of the speaker's proficiency.

An engaged listener.

7 Quotes by Cicero

Marcus Tullius Cicero was a Roman statesman, orator, lawyer, and philosopher, born in 106 BC in Arpinum, a hill town south of Rome. He is considered one of Rome's greatest orators and writers. He came from a wealthy family and rose to the highest office in the Republic, that of Consul, in 63 BC.

Cicero was not just a politician and orator but also a prolific writer on philosophy, adapting Greek models to create a Latin philosophical vocabulary for Roman application. In short, he made Hellenistic philosophy accessible to Romans. He wrote about political and legal theory, moral obligation, the nature of happiness, and the qualities of an ideal orator.

Cicero's career ended during the power struggles that followed Julius Caesar's death. He was executed in 43 BC. His writings on philosophy, politics, and rhetoric shaped the intellectual landscape of the Western world. His ideas on republicanism and the importance of law influenced Enlightenment thinkers and the men who framed the United States Constitution. His works remain fundamental to understanding Roman culture, law, and government.

Cicero believed in the importance of republicanism, civic duty, and the rule of law, advocating for a balanced government and ethical leadership based on moral obligation and virtue. He emphasized the power of reason and promoted the idea that good citizens should act for the common good, not personal gain.

Cicero, marble statue in front of the Old Palace of Justice in Rome

\#1

"Gratitude is not only the greatest of virtues, but the parent of all others." -Cicero

In Cicero's view, gratitude is the greatest virtue because it is a profound acknowledgement of the goodness others have provided; and it inspires a reciprocal desire to act virtuously in return. By recognizing and appreciating what others have done, gratitude fosters a sense of moral obligation and encourages a range of other virtuous behaviours, such as generosity, humility, and justice.

Thus, by calling gratitude the "parent" of all virtues, Cicero suggests that it gives rise to and nurtures other virtues. When one starts from a place of gratitude, it naturally leads to the cultivation of additional positive traits, creating a virtuous cycle that enhances personal ethics and societal harmony.

Gratitude.

#2

"Cannot people realize how large an income is thrift." -Cicero

Cicero is pointing out that many people overlook the value of saving in their pursuit of greater income. They fail to recognize that reducing expenses and managing resources wisely can secure financial stability and even prosperity. His observation encourages a reconsideration of how wealth is built and maintained, suggesting that wise management of one's existing assets is as crucial as the pursuit of new financial gains. This idea remains profoundly relevant today, emphasizing that financial prudence can lead to lasting economic benefits and should be valued as highly as increasing one's earnings.

Beyond merely being a commentary on financial management, it is possible that Cicero was also advocating for a simpler life with fewer complications, which in turn could lead to greater fulfillment and contentment. Think of all the free time you can unleash just by removing unnecessary complications from your life.

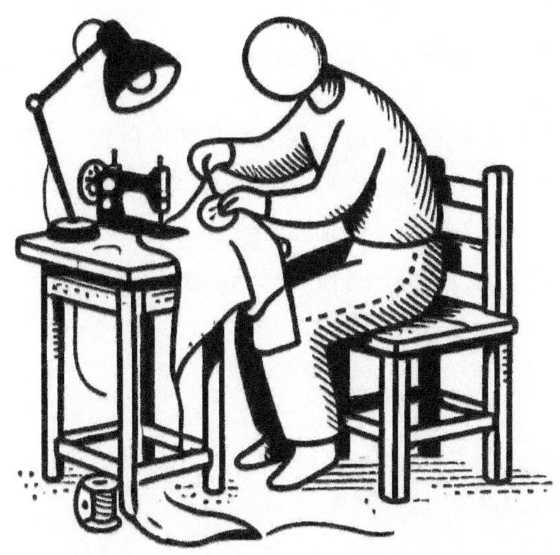

Thrift comes in many forms.

#3

"While there's life, there's hope." -Cicero

Oft quoted, Cicero's statement captures a timeless sentiment of optimism and perseverance. He offers the thought that as long as one is alive, opportunities for change, improvement, and success remain possible. The phrase suggests that life itself inherently holds potential. It encourages maintaining hope regardless of current circumstances.

This idea serves as a motivational reminder to not give up, even in the face of adversity or despair. Cicero suggests that the mere fact of being alive provides a foundation for optimism because new possibilities and solutions can emerge as long as one continues to engage with life's challenges. The saying encourages resilience and a forward-looking perspective, urging us to keep striving and believing in the potential for positive outcomes as long as we live.

While Cicero was not a Stoic, this perspective is particularly resonant in the context of Stoic philosophy, which values endurance and the continuous pursuit of virtue, regardless of what is happening around us. It's useful advice for the many people who might find themselves overwhelmed with no obvious relief in sight.

The cultivation of life is the cultivation of hope.

#4

"If you have a garden and a library, you have everything you need." -Cicero

This statement reflects the values of a well-rounded existence that combines the pleasures and tranquility of nature with the intellectual stimulation and wisdom offered by books.

The garden symbolizes a connection to nature, physical activity, and the simple, earthly pleasures that can ground a person and provide a sense of peace and self-sufficiency. It represents the nurturing of life and an appreciation for the natural world, which were important aspects of a balanced life in Cicero's view.

On the other hand, the library represents the realm of intellectual engagement, learning, and the cultural enrichment that books provide. It signifies the pursuit of knowledge and the development of the mind, which Cicero held in high regard.

Together, by feeding both the body and soul, we can achieve happiness and a complete life.

Completeness.

#5

"Politicians are not born; they are excreted." -Cicero

Cicero often commented on the ethical and moral deficiencies he observed in the political arena of ancient Rome. This particular remark uses some unpleasant imagery to suggest that politicians are not destined or naturally inclined to their roles through noble qualities. Rather, they emerge as a byproduct or waste of the political system.

Cicero alludes to a process of degradation rather than of noble birth, where the political system itself is portrayed as corrupting, producing leaders who are more a result of the system's flaws than of their own virtues. Like all the quotes collected in this volume, this insight from Cicero is as relevant today as it was in ancient Rome.

The venomous, duplicitous politician.

#6

"An unjust peace is better than a just war." -Cicero

Cicero suggests that the negative consequences of war, even one fought for just reasons, often outweigh the benefits of achieving justice through conflict. War brings destruction, suffering, and instability, affecting not only those directly involved but also broader society. In contrast, even an imperfect or unjust peace preserves life, maintains social order, and allows for the possibility of future improvements without the immediate cost of human lives and societal upheaval.

This is, of course, a controversial position, as many would argue that struggle and resistance are preferable to peace under an oppressive tyranny or other unpleasant conditions.

However, Cicero's quote underscores the idea that peace, even when flawed, provides a foundation for negotiation, dialogue, and gradual reform. An unjust peace can still offer opportunities for addressing grievances and achieving justice over time through non-violent means. By prioritizing peace, Cicero is advocating for the resolution of conflicts through diplomacy and compromise, emphasizing the long-term benefits of maintaining stability and harmony over the short-term satisfaction of waging a just war.

An imperfect peace after the toll of war.

#7

"There is nothing so absurd that some philosopher has not already said it." -Cicero

Cicero suggests that within the vast realm of philosophy, almost every conceivable idea, no matter how strange or seemingly absurd, has been explored by some philosopher. Philosophy, by its nature, encourages questioning and examining all aspects of life, reality, and existence, often leading to a wide array of theories and perspectives. This openness to exploring even the most unusual ideas is what drives philosophical progress and intellectual diversity. Cicero's statement acknowledges that philosophy does not shy away from considering ideas that may initially seem irrational or far-fetched.

Furthermore, Cicero's quote can be seen as a commentary on the boldness and creativity inherent in philosophical thought. Philosophers are willing to challenge conventional wisdom and propose theories that push the boundaries of accepted knowledge. This willingness to entertain and articulate unconventional ideas, even at the risk of appearing absurd, is a key aspect of philosophical exploration and debate. Thus, maybe Cicero is celebrating the value of philosophy in its ability to broaden our understanding and challenge our perceptions, even if it sometimes leads to seemingly absurd conclusions.

The absurdity of some oratory.

10 Quotes by Marcus Aurelius

THE NEXT THREE PHILOSOPHERS featured in this volume are all members of the school of philosophy called Stoicism. Founded in the early 3rd century BC by Zeno of Citium, Stoicism advocates for the development of self-control and fortitude as a means to overcome destructive emotions. Stoics argue that "virtue is sufficient for happiness", with the core virtues being wisdom, courage, justice, and temperance or self-restraint.

Stoicism was embraced in the 20th century by English-speaking psychotherapists. In 1979, Aaron Beck, the father of cognitive behavioural therapy (CBT), once wrote that "the philosophical origins of cognitive therapy can be traced back to the Stoic philosophers."

In addition to Zeno, the most notable classical Stoics are Seneca, Epictetus, Musonius, and Marcus Aurelius. But in modern times, Stoicism has roared back into popular fashion, notably among Silicon Valley entrepreneurs, due in large part to advocates like Ryan Holiday, who has written numerous popular books on the topic. Holiday often refers to Marcus Aurelius as "the wisest man in the world" for his ability to bear an extraordinary weight of responsibility with centeredness and philosophical calm.

Marcus Aurelius was a Roman emperor born in 121 AD. His reign from 161 AD until his death in 180 AD is often remembered both for the emperor's philosophical pursuits and for the challenges that he faced managing the empire during military conflicts and the Antonine Plague.

In philosophy, Marcus Aurelius is best known for his work "Meditations," a series of personal writings that record his ideas on Stoic philosophy. Those notes were never meant for public consumption, but for the emperor's own personal reflection, which makes the work all the more impressive. "Meditations" is remarkable for its insightful reflection on how to live virtuously and cope with internal and external conflicts. It is considered one of the greatest works of philosophy.

Marcus Aurelius believed strongly in his duty to lead and serve the Roman people, reflecting the Stoic commitment to virtue and the role one is given in life. He advocated for accepting things one cannot change, focusing on behaving correctly in the present, and using reason to navigate life's challenges. He emphasized achieving peace of mind through mastery over one's desires and fears, reflecting the Stoic belief that true happiness comes from within, not from external circumstances.

Marcus Aurelius is remembered both as a wise and effective emperor who dealt justly with his duties, and as a philosopher who contributed significantly to Stoicism. His writings continue to influence both academic and popular audiences. His perspectives on how to remain resilient in the face of physical and emotional pressures are invaluable in the modern context.

Bust of Emperor Marcus Aurelius, Musée Saint-Raymond, Toulouse, France

#1

"Reject your sense of injury and the injury itself disappears." - Marcus Aurelius

Emperor Marcus Aurelius was among the most prominent of Stoic philosophers. In this quote, he isn't suggesting that we ignore or trivialize our emotions. Instead, he is prompting us to question our automatic thoughts and responses. The statement is about cultivating emotional strength and balance, mastering the skill of detachment, and ensuring that external circumstances do not control our internal calm.

Any emotional suffering that we experience from being wronged often stems more from our perception of the event than from the event itself. By choosing to let go of our sense of being injured, we can mitigate or even eliminate the emotional impact of the injury.

Marcus Aurelius preferred to focus on the importance of personal agency in how he experienced and responded to life's challenges. The Stoics believed that our judgments and interpretations shape our reality. If we interpret an event as a grave injustice, we will feel the corresponding emotional turmoil. However, if we choose to see it as insignificant or unworthy of our emotional energy, the negative impact diminishes. This perspective encourages us to cultivate a mindset of detachment and rational assessment, allowing us to navigate adversities with greater equanimity and strength.

In essence, this quote is about the limitless power of perception.

Discarding the armour of hurt.

#2

"Do not act as if you were going to live ten thousand years. Death hangs over you. While you live, while it is in your power, be good." - Marcus Aurelius

With this statement, Emperor Marcus Aurelius reflects his desire not to procrastinate or delay living a good and moral life. He was mindful that death is always imminent. Therefore, because our time is limited and unpredictable, we should focus on living rightly and virtuously in the moment. In other words, we should not waste the limited time that we have.

While it is possible that Aurelius never meant for his writings to be shared widely, this perspective nevertheless motivates us not only to be mindful of our mortality but also to use that awareness as a catalyst to live ethically and meaningfully.

The urgency of living virtuously in the face of the inevitability of death.

#3

"It is not death that a man should fear, but he should fear never beginning to live." - Marcus Aurelius

Emperor Marcus Aurelius believed that one should not necessarily fear death, which is a natural and inevitable end that all must face. Rather, one should fear living a life that lacks purpose, depth, or virtue. From a Stoic perspective, a life well-lived involves pursuing wisdom, practicing ethical behaviour, and fulfilling one's roles and responsibilities with diligence and integrity.

The writings of Marcus Aurelius encourage us to focus on actively living in accordance with our values and principles, making the most of the present moment without undue anxiety about death. In this way, perhaps we can ensure that our time, however long or short, is spent meaningfully, rather than being wasted in avoidance or trivial pursuits. This idea challenges us to live fully and authentically, embracing life's experiences and striving for personal and moral growth.

Hesitation at the brink of life's journey.

#4

"The object of life is not to be on the side of the majority, but to escape finding oneself in the ranks of the insane." - Marcus Aurelius

This sentiment reflects the Stoic ideal of living according to reason and virtue rather than conforming to societal norms or popular opinions that may be misguided or irrational.

Emperor Marcus Aurelius uses the term "insane" metaphorically to describe behaviour that is irrational or devoid of reason, which he saw as contrary to the natural human capacity for rational thought. For Aurelius, the "insane" are those who live unexamined lives, driven by passions, desires, and external influences without thoughtful consideration of their actions or their consequences.

The goal, therefore, is to cultivate one's mind and character so thoroughly that one is not merely following others blindly but is instead guided by wisdom and reason. This involves a deliberate avoidance of the mass behaviour that characterizes much of human conduct, which can often lead to moral and philosophical confusion. Instead, he advocates for a life of thoughtful deliberation and self-guidance, aiming to achieve true fulfillment and peace within oneself.

Discernment and individuality.

#5

"You have power over your mind - not outside events. Realize this, and you will find strength." - Marcus Aurelius

This quote encapsulates a central tenet of Stoic philosophy: the distinction between what we can control and what we cannot. According to Stoicism, the path to peace and resilience lies in understanding and embracing this distinction.

Emperor Marcus Aurelius emphasizes that individuals have control over their own thoughts, reactions, and attitudes, but not over external circumstances or the actions of others. This perspective advises that strength and tranquility are achieved not by attempting to control the uncontrollable but by focusing on one's own mental and emotional responses.

By mastering one's internal state and choosing rational and positive responses, regardless of external situations, one cultivates a form of inner fortitude. Aurelius suggests that this realization itself is empowering—it liberates from the anxiety of trying to control the external world and redirects energy towards self-mastery, which is both achievable and deeply rewarding.

This insight encourages a form of proactive resilience, where one finds strength through internal consistency and virtue, regardless of external chaos or challenges. It is a call to cultivate inner resources that lead to enduring stability and peace.

Control over the mind amidst external chaos.

#6

"How much more grievous are the consequences of anger than the causes of it." - Marcus Aurelius

As a Stoic philosopher, Emperor Marcus Aurelius emphasized the importance of mastering one's emotions and maintaining rational control over one's reactions to external events. His reflection serves as a caution that while the triggers of anger might be minor or temporary, the repercussions of reacting in anger can be severe and long-lasting. These consequences might include damaged relationships, missed opportunities, or even long-term regret. Aurelius's wisdom encourages individuals to consider the broader impact of their emotional responses and to seek a calm, measured approach to life's challenges, focusing on rational thinking and self-control rather than yielding to impulsive emotions. This perspective not only aims to prevent unnecessary distress but also to promote a more peaceful and purposeful life.

The pointlessness of anger.

#7

"The best revenge is not to be like your enemy." - Marcus Aurelius

This quote conveys a powerful lesson on personal integrity and ethical conduct, reflective of Stoic philosophy. Emperor Marcus Aurelius is suggesting that the most effective way to counteract wrongdoing or malice from others is not through retaliation or sinking to their level, but by maintaining one's own higher standards of behaviour. Perhaps a modern version would be Michelle Obama's 2016 statement, "When they go low, we go high."

This idea emphasizes the importance of self-control and moral superiority. Instead of responding to negative actions with similar negativity, Marcus Aurelius advocates for embodying virtues that the enemy lacks, such as patience, kindness, and justice. By doing so, one not only avoids the moral corruption associated with revenge but also sets a positive example, potentially inspiring change in others or at least preserving one's own peace of mind and dignity.

In essence, Marcus Aurelius teaches that true strength lies in resisting the impulse to retaliate, choosing instead a path defined by virtue and resilience. This approach not only distances oneself from the destructive emotions and behaviours of adversaries but also reinforces one's commitment to living a principled and honourable life.

Aggression vs openness.

\#8

"When you arise in the morning, think of what a privilege it is to be alive, to think, to enjoy, to love ..." - Marcus Aurelius

This quote emphasizes the value and significance of everyday moments and the simple yet profound act of being alive. As a Stoic philosopher, Emperor Marcus Aurelius often focused on gratitude and mindfulness, encouraging a deep appreciation for the present and the basic elements of human existence.

The statement is an invitation to start each day with a sense of gratitude and wonder about the opportunities that life offers, such as the ability to think, experience joy, and feel love. Aurelius saw these aspects not just as incidental parts of life, but as profound blessings that deserve recognition and appreciation.

The practice recommended in this quote embodies Stoic ideals of mindfulness, gratitude, and the pursuit of virtue. It's a reminder to not take life for granted and to live each day with intention and appreciation.

Gratefully embrace the new day.

#9

"The universe is change, and life mere opinion." - Marcus Aurelius

Emperor Marcus Aurelius, a prominent Stoic, suggests that change is the fundamental nature of the universe. Everything in existence is in a constant state of flux, from the smallest particles to the vast cosmic structures. This acknowledgment of perpetual change encourages a perspective of acceptance and adaptability. By recognizing that change is inevitable, perhaps we can learn to embrace it rather than resist it, understanding that it is a natural and integral part of life. The Stoics generally advocated for accepting the natural order of things and focusing on what is within our control.

The second part of the quote, "life mere opinion," reminds us of the subjective nature of human experience. According to Aurelius, much of what we consider reality is shaped by our perceptions, judgments, and beliefs. Our opinions about events, people, and circumstances color our experience of life. This means that our mental and emotional responses are often more about our internal interpretations than the external events themselves. By recognizing this, we can strive to develop a more rational and detached perspective, reducing unnecessary suffering caused by misguided opinions. Perhaps this can help us to foster a more balanced and serene approach to life's challenges.

External things are neither good nor bad. We just judge them to be so. The Stoics argue that such judgement is ultimately a choice. Reading about conflicts or existential threats in the news can be worrying. But it is within our individual power to choose whether or not to let such news change our mood or demeanour.

Contemplate change.

#10

"The happiness of your life depends upon the quality of your thoughts." - Marcus Aurelius

Emperor Marcus Aurelius suggests that our internal thoughts and attitudes play a critical role in determining our happiness. The quality of our thoughts—whether they are positive, rational, and constructive or negative, irrational, and destructive—directly impacts how we perceive and experience life. According to Stoic philosophy, external circumstances are often beyond our control. But we can control our responses to them through our thoughts. By cultivating a mindset that focuses on virtues, rationality, and positivity, we can enhance our sense of well-being and happiness regardless of external conditions.

Furthermore, Aurelius' quote underscores the Stoic practice of self-examination and mental discipline. By being mindful of the nature and quality of our thoughts, we can consciously choose to develop healthier and more constructive thinking patterns. This involves challenging negative or irrational beliefs, practicing gratitude, and maintaining a balanced perspective. Through this mental discipline, individuals can create a more resilient and contented state of mind, leading to a happier and more fulfilling life.

In essence, Aurelius reminds us of the power of our inner world to shape our experience of happiness, advocating for intentional and thoughtful cultivation of our mental landscape. In other words, regardless of what is happening in our world, we have it in our power to construct internal happiness.

The cultivation of thought.

8 Quotes by Seneca

Lucius Annaeus Seneca, or Seneca the Younger, also commonly known simply as Seneca, was a Roman Stoic philosopher, statesman, and playwright who lived from approximately 4 BC to AD 65. He is considered one of the most important and complex Stoic philosophers, whose life and writings profoundly influenced the development of the field of ethics.

He was born in what is now Córdoba, Spain, and brought to Rome for education in rhetoric and philosophy. Rising to prominence in Roman political circles, he became an advisor to the infamous Emperor Nero, initially serving as his tutor and later his chief minister. He eventually died by court-ordered suicide, after having been accused of conspiring against Nero.

Seneca's philosophical writings are extensive and include essays, letters, and tragedies that explore Stoic doctrine and ethics. His letters to his friend Lucilius are a cornerstone of Stoic thought and discuss moral and ethical questions, personal anecdotes, and philosophical reasoning.

Seneca's writings considered practical approaches to ethical living, the importance of rational control over emotions, and the acceptance of fate. His ideas on the brevity of life and the importance of living virtuously have resonated through centuries, influencing not just philosophical thought but also literature and broader culture. His perspectives on virtue, the nature of happiness, and the importance of living according to nature have influenced Christian ethics and moral philosophy. In essence, he argued that the pursuit of wisdom is the best path to true happiness.

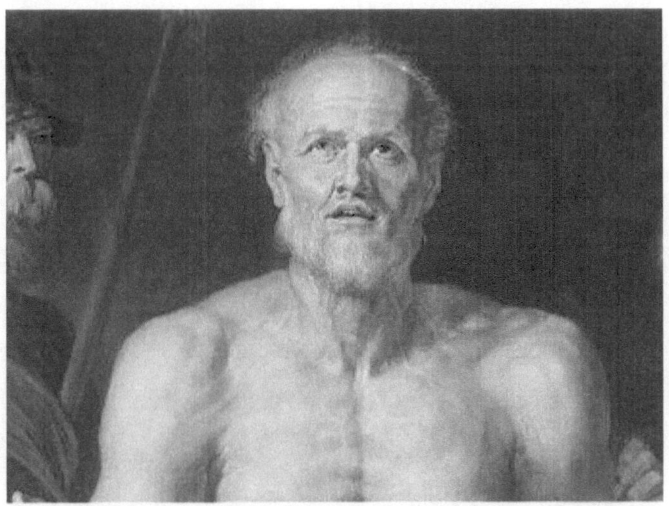

Cropped from The Death of Seneca, by Peter Paul Rubens, c.1614, Alte Pinakothek, Munich

\#1

"No man was ever wise by chance." -Seneca

According to Seneca, acquiring wisdom requires a conscious and intentional pursuit. This involves engaging in philosophical study, learning from one's experiences, practicing self-discipline, and constantly reflecting on one's actions and their consequences. Wisdom is cultivated through persistent and thoughtful effort over time, rather than being a trait that someone might simply stumble upon or possess without effort.

In essence, Seneca is highlighting that becoming wise is a process that demands dedication and purposeful living. It is an achievement that comes from actively seeking knowledge and understanding, and from applying those insights to improve oneself and navigate life more effectively.

The hard work of wisdom.

#2

"If you live according to nature, you will never be poor. If you live according to opinion, you will never be rich." -Seneca

This quote encapsulates a central Stoic philosophy about simplicity and independence from societal expectations. Here, natural living refers to aligning one's life with essential and natural needs, emphasizing simplicity, self-sufficiency, and virtue. According to Seneca, by focusing on what is truly necessary and natural—like contentment, virtue, and basic needs—one avoids unnecessary desires and dependencies.

Conversely, allowing the opinions of others to dictate much of one's attitudes and behaviours can lead to a life governed by external perceptions, societal norms, and the pursuit of wealth and status. Seneca argues that such an existence, driven by the endless quest for approval and accumulation, inevitably leads to a kind of poverty, where one is never satisfied or truly wealthy regardless of accumulated riches. Seneca opposes the relentless pursuit of material wealth at the expense of inner richness and advocates for a life rooted in Stoic values of independence, virtue, and contentment with one's state.

Eschew a life governed by societal opinions and material desires.

#3

"All cruelty springs from weakness." -Seneca

As a Stoic, Seneca believed that virtues such as wisdom, courage, justice, and temperance should be regarded as strengths. Failing to embody these virtues is thus seen as a form of moral weakness. The Stoic ideal is rational self-control and moral integrity. They believed that when individuals are cruel, it is often because they lack the strength to cope with their own fears, insecurities, or inadequacies in a constructive manner. Instead of addressing their weaknesses and working towards personal improvement, they might project these insecurities onto others in the form of aggression or cruelty.

This sentiment is, in many ways, at the heart of bullying. Seneca's lesson is therefore a vital one for modern life, where new avenues like social media have created opportunities for the morally weak to express cruelty.

Seneca believed that the remedy to cruelty lies in the cultivation of virtue and inner strength, enabling individuals to respond to life's challenges with understanding and compassion rather than with harmful actions.

It is often the morally unsure who resort to pointless aggression and cruelty.

\#4

"Sometimes even to live is an act of courage."-Seneca

Seneca recognizes that life can be incredibly difficult and filled with suffering, pain, and adversity. There are moments when the burdens and struggles of existence can feel overwhelming, whether due to personal loss, illness, societal pressures, or existential despair. In such times, continuing to live and face these challenges head-on requires immense courage. Seneca is acknowledging the strength and resilience needed to persist through life's darkest moments, highlighting that simply choosing to keep going in the face of overwhelming odds is a testament to one's inner fortitude and bravery.

Furthermore, Seneca's quote aligns with Stoic philosophy, which teaches the importance of enduring hardships with dignity and maintaining one's virtue despite external circumstances. The Stoics believed in the power of the human spirit to withstand and overcome adversity through reason, self-control, and acceptance of what cannot be changed. By framing the act of living as an act of courage, Seneca emphasizes the value of perseverance and the noble struggle to live a meaningful life, even when it is incredibly challenging. This perspective encourages individuals to recognize their own strength and to find courage in their daily existence, regardless of the obstacles they may face.

The courage of living.

#5

"It is not the man who has too little, but the man who craves more, that is poor." -Seneca

According to Seneca, true poverty stems not from a lack of material possessions, but from unending desire and dissatisfaction with what one has. This perspective emphasizes that wealth and abundance lie in one's attitude and mindset rather than in physical resources.

The essence of Seneca's thought is that an insatiable appetite for more—whether it be money, status, or possessions—leads to a perpetual state of wanting and unhappiness, which he equates with real poverty. In contrast, a person who can find contentment with his or her current circumstances, regardless of how modest, is truly rich because that person is free from the unrest and turmoil of constant desire.

Seneca was a Stoic. Stoicism encourages self-sufficiency, moderation, and the cultivation of an inner sense of satisfaction, advocating for a life where happiness is not dependent on external acquisitions but on inner peace and fulfillment.

Contentment does not depend on wealth.

#6

"We suffer more often in imagination than in reality." -Seneca

As a Stoic, Seneca believed that much of our suffering arises not from our actual circumstances, but from our perceptions and fears about those circumstances. This concept is integral to Stoic thought, which teaches that our reactions to events are the true source of distress, not the events themselves.

In this quote, Seneca is saying that people frequently torment themselves with worries about potential negative outcomes, disasters, or misfortunes that may never actually occur. These imagined scenarios can cause significant emotional turmoil, often more intense than what is experienced in dealing with real issues.

In essence, he is pointing out that the mind has a capacity to create its own suffering through negative anticipation and catastrophic thinking. This is a tendency that is all too common today.

Seneca's observation encourages a focus on managing one's thoughts and responses, advocating for a rational and present-focused mindset that assesses and deals with reality as it is, rather than becoming entangled in unfounded fears and speculations. This way of thinking promotes mental resilience, reducing unnecessary emotional suffering by aligning one's reactions more closely with actual, rather than imagined, experiences.

The undisciplined nature of imagination.

#7

"Associate with people who are likely to improve you."
-Seneca

By surrounding ourselves with individuals who are wise, virtuous, and committed to good principles, we are more likely to adopt these traits ourselves. These relationships can challenge us to think critically, act ethically, and strive for a better version of ourselves. In essence, our social environment can either uplift us or pull us down, and Seneca advises choosing associations that lead to the elevation and enrichment of our character.

This counsel not only aims at personal betterment but also at contributing positively to the community and society by reinforcing constructive and supportive social networks, an action that is well known to promote overall happiness and contentment.

Seek mentors and colleagues who challenge us intellectually and encourage us to take on new challenges.

"Luck is what happens when preparation meets opportunity." -Seneca

This statement conveys the idea that what many people perceive as luck is not merely a product of random chance, but often the result of diligent preparation and being ready to seize opportunities when they arise.

In this view, Seneca emphasizes that success is largely influenced by our readiness to act and make the most of circumstances that come our way. By preparing ourselves—through education, training, and thoughtful planning—we position ourselves to take advantage of opportunities that might otherwise seem like fortuitous events. Essentially, Seneca argues that by being well-prepared, we can transform potential opportunities into "luck." This perspective encourages proactive behaviour and underscores the importance of personal responsibility in crafting one's fate, rather than relying solely on the whims of chance.

Taking proactive steps to increase our probability of success.

30 Quotes by Epictetus

EPICTETUS WAS BORN AROUND 50 AD in Hierapolis, Phrygia, in present-day Turkey. A Greek, he spent his early life as a slave in Rome, which profoundly shaped his philosophical views. Epictetus is known for his focus on ethics and on advocating for control over one's emotions.

Although born a slave, Epictetus was eventually freed and went on to teach philosophy in Rome until 93 AD, when Emperor Domitian banished all philosophers from the city. He then settled in Nicopolis, in northwestern Greece, where he established his own school. It was said that tortures he endured while a slave left him disabled and dependent on a crutch for walking; though, it is possible that he had been disabled since birth.

Perhaps inspired in part by his experience with his own physical disability and low social status, Epictetus's philosophy concerned the acceptance what one cannot change while focusing efforts on what one can control. Like other Stoics, Epictetus believed that virtue is the highest good and that everything else, such as wealth, health, and reputation, should be regarded as indifferent. Virtue alone leads to true happiness.

Epictetus's Stoic teachings have endured through the centuries, influencing a wide range of thinkers and leaders from Marcus Aurelius to modern self-help gurus. His emphasis on personal responsibility and the value of inner freedom has made his work relevant to contemporary discussions about the philosophy of psychological resilience, so relevance to the youth of today.

Illustration of Epictetus, with lamp and crutch, in Edward Ivie's 1715 Latin translation of the Enchiridion.

\#1

"People are not disturbed by things, but by the views they take of them." -Epictetus

This is a core principle of Stoic philosophy that focuses on the role of perception in human experience. According to Epictetus, it is not external events or situations themselves that cause us distress or happiness; rather, it is how we interpret and react to these events.

This idea emphasizes that our emotional and mental disturbances arise from our judgments and beliefs about what happens around us, not from the events themselves. For instance, two individuals might experience the same setback or challenge, yet their emotional responses could be vastly different depending on how they perceive and think about the situation.

By recognizing that our thoughts and beliefs shape our reactions, Epictetus advocates for gaining control over our perceptions and responses. The goal is to cultivate a mindset that views situations objectively and responds to them with rationality and calmness. This approach not only minimizes unnecessary suffering but also empowers us to maintain our tranquility and happiness regardless of external circumstances.

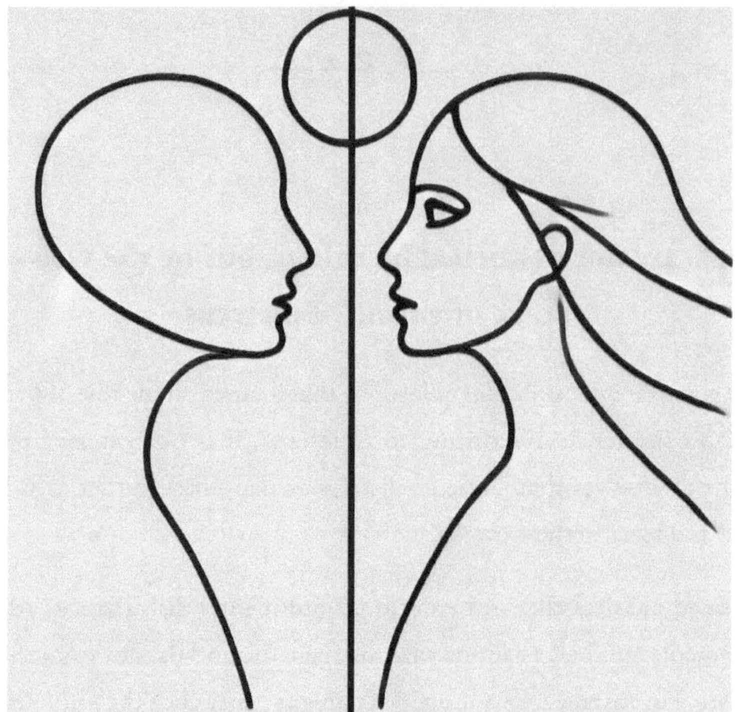

One's internal reality is shaped by one's view of things.

#2

"Wealth consists not in having great possessions, but in having few wants." -Epictetus

Real richness comes from simplicity and self-sufficiency, rather than from the accumulation of material goods. According to Epictetus, the key to wealth is minimizing desires to what is necessary and to what is within one's control. By reducing one's wants, an individual achieves a form of freedom and contentment that is not vulnerable to external circumstances or changes.

Epictetus argues that by focusing on limiting our desires and being content with less, we can attain a more profound and stable form of happiness. Such wealth is characterized by inner peace that leads to a life that is not dictated by the endless acquisition of goods.

*Despite accumulating many possessions,
fulfillment remains absent.*

#3

"If you want to improve, be content to be thought foolish and stupid." -Epictetus

This quote addresses a common obstacle in personal development: the fear of others' opinions. This Stoic idea encourages embracing humility and the willingness to appear ignorant or unwise as part of the learning process.

The underlying message is that true improvement often requires us to step out of our comfort zone, to ask questions, and make mistakes. These are all actions that might lead others to mistakenly perceive us as foolish or uninformed. Epictetus suggests that a genuine commitment to personal growth may necessitate enduring such criticism or misperception from others who might not understand or appreciate your path. It's an important observation in this modern era of social media and instant judgement.

According to this philosophy, we must prioritize our development over maintaining a facade of competence or intelligence. By disregarding external judgments, we can focus on self-improvement without hindrance. Epictetus is emphasizing that if we are truly devoted to becoming better, we must be willing to face and accept temporary perceptions of foolishness as a necessary part of the journey toward wisdom and self-mastery.

The path to wisdom often requires enduring the mockery of those who do not understand the path.

#4

"The key is to keep company only with people who uplift you, whose presence calls forth your best." -Epictetus

Epictetus suggests that the people with whom we associate have a significant impact on our personal development. Being around those who uplift us and encourage our best qualities can foster our growth, helping us to embody virtues such as courage, honesty, and integrity. Conversely, spending time with individuals who bring out our negative traits or discourage our progress can hinder our development.

It's unsurprising that this particular sentiment from Epictetus resembles a quote from his fellow Stoic Seneca, who had written decades earlier, "Associate with people who are likely to improve you."

This advice encourages us to be selective about our associations, seeking out relationships that are supportive, inspiring, and conducive to our betterment. This approach not only enhances our ability to live according to our values but also strengthens our capacity to contribute positively to the lives of others.

We are either constrained or uplifted by the company we keep.

#5

"Only the educated are free." -Epictetus

This quote is, of course, a favourite among educators. According to Epictetus, real freedom is achieved not through external circumstances, such as wealth or social status, but through the mind's mastery over itself. Being educated, in his view, means having the intellectual tools to examine and control one's responses to external events, to differentiate between what is within one's control and what is not, and to adhere to rational and virtuous principles despite external pressures.

This concept of education is about cultivating an inner resilience and autonomy that allows one to remain undisturbed by external disturbances. It entails a thorough understanding of human nature and the workings of the universe, leading to a life governed by reason rather than by impulse or societal influences. For Epictetus, the truly free individuals are the ones who have mastered themselves through philosophy, making educated decisions based on wisdom and virtue.

Even shackles do not slow the march to wisdom.

#6

"Do not try to seem wise to others." -Epictetus

Epictetus was a Stoic, which means he prized authenticity and self-improvement above external validation or social status. By advising not to attempt to appear wise, Epictetus is cautioning against the vanity and superficiality of seeking approval and admiration for one's intellectual or philosophical prowess. Such behaviour can lead to arrogance and may distract from the true purpose of wisdom, which is to guide one's own life and decisions effectively, not to impress others.

This statement also encourages focusing on personal growth and true understanding rather than on the perception of others. Epictetus suggests that genuine wisdom involves introspection, self-discipline, and the practice of virtue in one's life, irrespective of recognition or reward. This self-sufficiency is a key aspect of freedom and happiness in Stoic thought, as it liberates individuals from dependence on others' opinions and affirms the value of living according to one's principles.

True wisdom resides in not seeking to be performatively wise.

#7

"You are a little soul carrying around a corpse." -Epictetus

The quote reflects the Stoic view of the relationship between the mind (or soul) and the body. It metaphorically reflects the Stoic belief that the true essence of each of us is our rational soul, while our bodies are merely temporary, mortal vessels. The soul in the case is our capacity for reason and moral judgment.

Epictetus was a slave. Yet he argued that whether or not one is a slave has nothing to do with one's state of freedom. Given the temporal nature of physical life, neither our bodies nor our physical property are our own. By likening the body to a "corpse," Epictetus emphasizes its impermanence and the fact that it is subject to decay and death. This dramatic imagery reminds us that physical concerns, including pleasure, pain, and even life itself, are transient and should not dominate our thoughts and actions. The soul, in contrast, is portrayed as enduring and more significant, capable of reason and ethical living.

This perspective encourages a focus on cultivating virtues and moral integrity, which are within the control of the soul, rather than overly fixating on physical desires or fears about bodily suffering. It's a call to prioritize spiritual and intellectual growth, viewing the body as an instrument or tool to be used in the pursuit of a virtuous life, rather than the primary focus of one's existence.

The rational soul is the true self.

#8

"First say to yourself what you would be; and then do what you have to do." -Epictetus

By advising to first define what you want to be or become, Epictetus underscores the necessity of having a clear vision of your ideal self. He believed that this vision should align with Stoic virtues such as wisdom, courage, justice, and self-discipline. Knowing what you aspire to be sets a direction for your actions and decisions, guiding you toward personal growth and ethical living.

The second part of the statement, "do what you have to do," stresses the importance of taking concrete, disciplined actions that align with this vision. It's not enough to merely wish or dream about the kind of person you want to be; you must actively work towards this goal through consistent, purposeful behaviours.

This quote, therefore, is a call to deliberate and principled living, where one's actions are a reflection of one's deeper values and goals. It encourages a proactive approach to personal development, where self-reflection leads directly to purposeful action.

The application to modern life is obvious. When pursuing physical fitness, for example, it is useful to first define an achievable goal, such as a quantifiable amount of weight to lose or an amount of weight to lift, then develop a program to reach that goal. Career aspirations, financial ambitions, or educational paths are similarly considered.

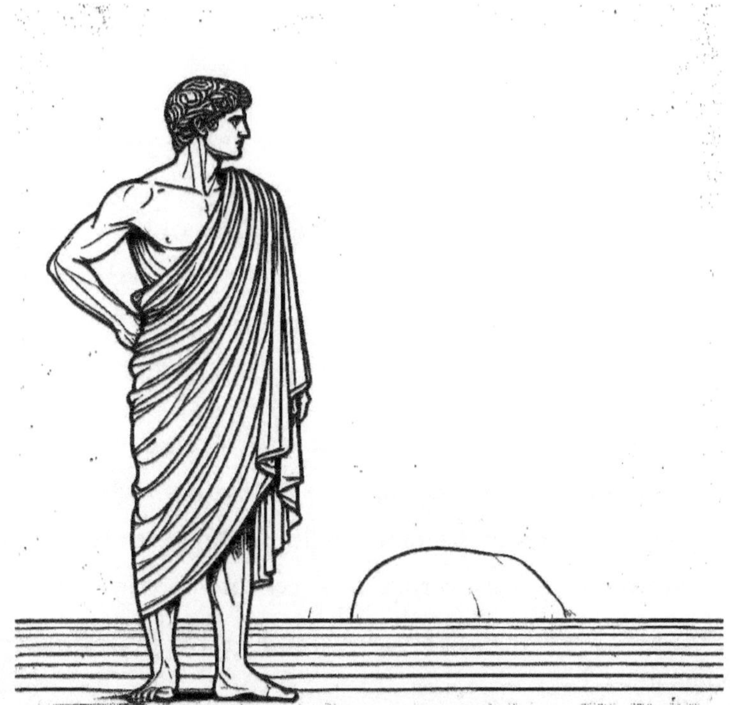

The contemplation of what and who one wishes to be.

#9

"Don't explain your philosophy. Embody it." -Epictetus

As a Stoic, Epictetus preached that one should not merely talk about virtues and wise living, but should actively demonstrate these qualities through actions. In other words, more colloquially, "talk is cheap."

This advice emphasizes the importance of actions over words. Epictetus is urging us to practice what we preach, to "walk the talk", and to make our lives a living example of our philosophical principles. It's an admonition against the empty boasting of knowledge without corresponding behaviour, which he saw as a common failing.

By embodying one's philosophy, a person not only provides a real-world example of its applicability and value but also deepens their own understanding and commitment to these principles. This approach aligns with the Stoic emphasis on virtue as something that must be practiced and manifested in daily life, not just discussed or studied. It's about living in such a way that your philosophy is apparent through your actions and way of being in the world.

In contemporary life, "walking the talk" prevents hypocrisy and allows for a less conflicted mindset. Consider a physical fitness coach who is unfit, or an environmental advocate who flagrantly pollutes. While can such individuals might be perceived as less trustworthy, the larger concern is for the shallowness of their principles and what it might mean for the depth of their contentment and fulfillment in life.

*Performing an act of kindness is better than
pontificating about kindness.*

#10

"Remember, it is not enough to be hit or insulted to be harmed, you must believe that you are being harmed. If someone succeeds in provoking you, realize that your mind is complicit in the provocation. Which is why it is essential that we not respond impulsively to impressions; take a moment before reacting, and you will find it easier to maintain control." -Epictetus

Epictetus's statement delves deep into the Stoic view of emotional control and perception. It highlights personal responsibility in emotional reactions. This suggests that if you feel provoked, it's because your own judgments or beliefs about the situation allow you to feel that way.

The advice to eschew impulsive reactions in favour of reflexive pause is a practical application of this philosophy. This pause provides an opportunity to assess the situation rationally, rather than reacting based on initial feelings or mistaken judgments. By doing so, you maintain control over your reactions, thereby reducing unnecessary suffering and enhancing your ability to act in accordance with reason and virtue.

A modern application would be in the chaotic and brazen world of social media, where every participant is well advised to realize that they are each complicit in any offence they might perceive.

In this sentiment, Epictetus reminds us of the importance of self-awareness and control in achieving inner peace and resilience, advocating for a reflective rather than reactive approach to life's challenges. This is a core component of Stoic training, aimed at fostering a life where one's happiness and peace are not at the mercy of external circumstances or other people's actions.

Choosing not to be offended.

\#11

"Circumstances don't make the man. They only reveal him to himself." -Epictetus

According to Epictetus, our reactions and choices in the face of external circumstances are what define our character, not the circumstances themselves. This idea suggests that while we cannot always control what happens to us, we can control how we respond. These responses reveal our true nature and virtues. This is a recurring message in Stoic philosophy.

In simpler terms, difficult or challenging situations don't create a person's character; they merely expose what was already there. This perspective encourages self-reflection and urges individuals to cultivate resilience, wisdom, and integrity, focusing on personal growth and ethical living regardless of external events.

How do we deal with difficulties? Do we see them as obstacles or opportunities? A viral video by podcaster and former Navy SEAL Jocko Willink reveals how Willink embraced this bit of Stoicism in his own world. In the video, Willink says that whenever a setback was brought to his attention, his response was, "Good." Instead of viewing obstacles as inherently negative, he chose to instead view them as opportunities for learning and improvement.

Challenges and adversity bring out inherent qualities, revealing who a person truly is under pressure. The goal, therefore, is not necessarily to avoid such challenges, but to strengthen one's underlying character to be more resilient against such challenges.

Adversity is a mirror revealing the true self.

#12

"Know, first, who you are, and then adorn yourself accordingly." -Epictetus

This quote underscores a fundamental Stoic principle: the importance of self-awareness and authenticity in one's actions and lifestyle choices. It encourages introspection and self-understanding as the basis for how one should present and conduct oneself in the world.

Though this quote has been used in fashion advertising, the idea of adornment refers not just to physical appearance but broadly to how one chooses to behave, speak, and interact with others based on an accurate understanding of one's true nature. Epictetus believed that knowing oneself deeply helps in identifying personal values and virtues. This self-knowledge then informs how one should conduct oneself, ensuring that external actions are in harmony with internal values.

In practical terms, Epictetus is advising that before you decide how to live, what roles to take on, or how to react in various situations, you should first understand your strengths, weaknesses, values, and goals. This alignment between inner understanding and outer actions is key to living a fulfilled and coherent life according to Stoic philosophy.

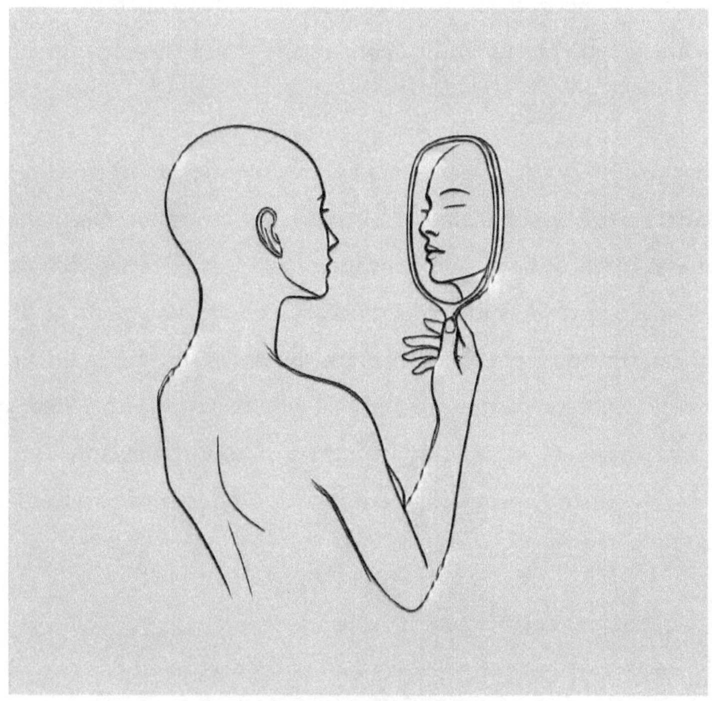

Knowledge of self is primary.

#13

"There is only one way to happiness and that is to cease worrying about things which are beyond the power or our will." -Epictetus

According to Epictetus, happiness is achievable by understanding and accepting the limits of our personal agency. The things within our control typically include our own thoughts, attitudes, and actions. On the other hand, external events—such as the behaviour of others, natural occurrences, or societal changes—are beyond our individual control and should not be sources of worry or distress.

By advising to cease worrying about these externalities, Epictetus suggests that undue concern for uncontrollable factors leads to unnecessary anxiety and unhappiness. Instead, he promotes the cultivation of inner virtues, such as wisdom, justice, courage, and temperance, which are all aspects of life that an individual can directly influence. Through this focus, we can maintain serenity and achieve happiness regardless of external circumstances. This Stoic approach aims to empower us by redirecting our energies towards personal growth and ethical living, in this way providing a pathway to a contented and fulfilling life.

Worrying is unproductive.

#14

"Small-minded people blame others. Average people blame themselves. The wise see all blame as foolishness."
-Epictetus

This statement explores the varying approaches that people often take towards adversity and accountability. Epictetus points out that the less mature tend to externalize their issues by blaming circumstances or other people, thereby avoiding personal accountability and self-reflection. This tendency prevents them from learning from their experiences and growing.

On the other hand, those who are more reflective might blame themselves, showing a higher level of personal responsibility but potentially succumbing to unhelpful self-criticism and guilt. The wise, according to Epictetus, rise above the habit of blaming altogether, recognizing it as counterproductive. They focus instead on understanding and learning from each situation, which equips them to handle future challenges more effectively. This mindset, central to Stoic philosophy, emphasizes controlling one's own responses and actions rather than getting entangled in blame, fostering resilience and personal growth.

Blame is counterproductive.

#15

"What really frightens and dismays us is not external events themselves, but the way in which we think about them. It is not things that disturb us, but our interpretation of their significance." -Epictetus

According to Epictetus, it's our interpretations or judgments about what happens, rather than the actual events, that evoke feelings of fear, dismay, or disturbance. For instance, losing a job can be viewed as a disaster or an opportunity, depending on one's perspective. If perceived as a disaster, it leads to distress. But if seen as an opportunity, it might be motivating.

This viewpoint represents a powerful form of psychological resilience. By changing how we interpret events, we can control our emotional responses. Thus, Epictetus advocates for a focus on examining and potentially altering our beliefs and judgments about external circumstances to maintain tranquility and emotional well-being.

This approach is empowering, suggesting that through disciplined thinking, one can maintain peace of mind regardless of the external chaos. Perhaps there is no better advice in these times of increasing uncertainty.

Consider someone who is apprehensive about speaking in front of a large crowd. But in actuality, the crowd poses no threat. The fear is in being judged negatively by the audience: something that is entirely imagined. It is therefore within the speaker's power to change that mindset. She can choose to reinterpret the event as a chance to share knowledge or to connect with others. In that way, she might find it less daunting and more rewarding.

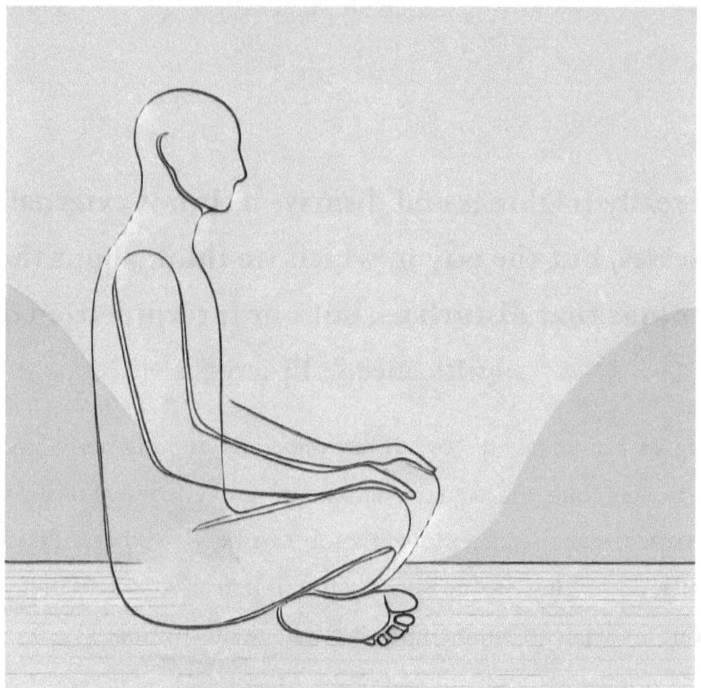

Stoic acceptance and internal control over external circumstances.

#16

"Don't seek to have events happen as you wish, but wish them to happen as they do happen, and all will be well with you."
-Epictetus

The idea here is to cultivate an attitude of acceptance toward the inevitability of events that are outside our control. By aligning our wishes with the actual course of events, we reduce emotional distress, which arises from expectations. Stoics believed that this leads to a more serene and contented life, as we are not constantly battling against the tide of circumstance but are instead flowing with it.

In practice, this means focusing on our responses and attitudes towards events, rather than the events themselves. This mindset shift helps build resilience and a stable sense of well-being, as it encourages us to focus on the elements of our lives over which we have influence and to let go of distress over those we cannot change. By doing so, we maintain our inner peace and capacity for happiness regardless of external conditions.

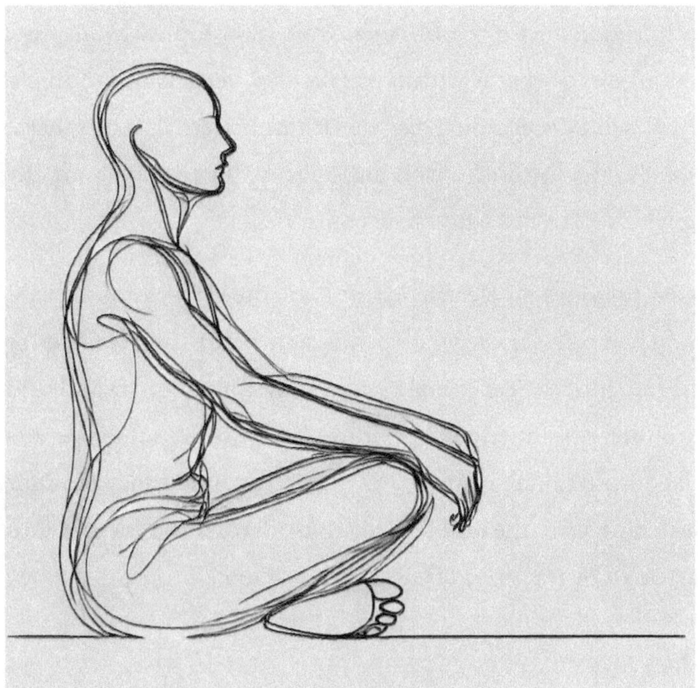

Acceptance and serenity.

\#17

"You become what you give your attention to." -Epictetus

According to Epictetus, our thoughts, actions, and ultimately, our very identity, are shaped by what we consistently direct our attention towards.

If we focus on negative or trivial matters, this can lead to the cultivation of negative traits or a shallow existence. Conversely, if we dedicate attention to positive, virtuous, and meaningful pursuits, we then foster personal growth and the development of a virtuous character.

This principle aligns with the broader Stoic philosophy, which advocates for mindful attention to what is within our control, such as our thoughts, actions, and attitudes, while disregarding distractions and external factors that are beyond our control. Essentially, Epictetus is highlighting the power of intentional focus in shaping who we are and what we become.

Social media provides an electric example of the application of this lesson to contemporary life. A person who spends significant time consuming negative or sensational content on social media may find their mood and outlook becoming more pessimistic or anxious. Conversely, someone who follows educational, inspirational, comedic, or uplifting content may feel more positive and motivated. Beware the online algorithms that send us deeper into the wells of despair, fueled by the truth of this timeless quote.

The flame of personal growth stoked by focused attention.

#18

"It's not what happens to you, but how you react to it that matters." -Epictetus

This quote encapsulates a core principle of Stoic philosophy: the focus on internal responses rather than external events. According to Epictetus, we have limited control over external circumstances and events, but we have complete control over our reactions, attitudes, and perceptions.

This idea emphasizes personal responsibility and the power of perspective. External events are often beyond our control since they happen to us without our choosing. However, we have the power to choose how we interpret and respond to these events. Our reactions can determine our emotional state and overall well-being. By maintaining a rational and composed mindset, we can navigate challenges more effectively and preserve our inner peace.

Epictetus advocates for cultivating a mindset that prioritizes inner virtues and rational responses. This approach empowers individuals to handle adversity with resilience and grace, fostering a sense of agency and stability regardless of external conditions. Ultimately, it is our reactions, shaped by our attitudes and beliefs, that define our experiences and the quality of our lives.

Acceptance and resilience in the face of adversity.

#19

"Man is not worried by real problems so much as by his imagined anxieties about real problems." -Epictetus

Epictetus implores us to remember the distinction between external events and our internal interpretations of those events. Real problems, such as health issues, financial difficulties, or personal conflicts, certainly present challenges. However, it is our tendency to exaggerate, catastrophize, and dwell on these problems in our minds that amplifies our distress. The imagined anxieties are the product of our thoughts, anticipations, and worst-case scenarios that we create, which often turn out to be more debilitating than the problems themselves.

Someone in a relationship might misinterpret a partner's busy schedule or distracted behaviour as disinterest or dissatisfaction. These imagined problems can cause unnecessary strain on the relationship, fueled by worries that may not reflect the partner's true feelings or intentions.

Epictetus is urging us to recognize the power of our thoughts in shaping our emotional responses. By managing our thoughts and focusing on rational, constructive perspectives, we can mitigate unnecessary anxiety and approach real problems with a clearer, calmer mind. This approach aligns with the broader Stoic goal of achieving tranquility and resilience through mindful control over one's perceptions and reactions.

Beware imagined anxieties.

#20

"Seek not the good in external things; seek it in yourselves."
-Epictetus

In Stoicism, external goods such as wealth, status, and physical pleasures are considered unimportant. They neither contribute to nor detract from true happiness. Instead, the Stoics argue that virtue is the sole good and is entirely dependent on one's own actions and character.

To the Stoics, virtue is defined by qualities like wisdom, justice, courage, and moderation. By focusing on cultivating these internal virtues, we can achieve a state of equanimity and resilience, regardless of external circumstances.

For example, a person might derive satisfaction from the process of learning itself, appreciating the intellectual growth and insights gained, rather than external outcomes like grades or degrees. Or, rather than obsessing over appearance or what others think of our fitness regime, we are better advised to concentrate on how better lifestyle choices make us healthier.

This perspective encourages personal responsibility and self-improvement, suggesting that we have the power to create our own good by developing our character and choosing virtuous actions, rather than relying on the external world to provide happiness or fulfillment.

The emptiness of wealth and social status.

#21

"We have two ears and one mouth so that we can listen twice as much as we speak." -Epictetus

This famous aphorism is often attributed to Epictetus. But it is possible that he did not write these words. Even so, the sentiment aligns with his general philosophy. He certainly advocated for the virtues of self-control and the careful consideration of one's words.

Of course, the quote suggests that listening is at least as important as speaking, and is possibly more important. Indeed, a greater focus should be placed on understanding others rather than on being heard oneself. This approach increases the probability of learning and understanding, of being empathetic and building better relationships, and of building the capacity to resolve conflicts.

Of relevance to the Stoic way of thinking, prioritizing listening over speaking also contributes to the nurturing of self-control and temperance, in that one must resist one's urges and desires to be heard, in order to accentuate the needs of others.

Communication is not just about voicing one's own thoughts but also about being open to and absorbing what others have to say. Again, this is a lesson that the modern world needs to absorb, with our current obsession with platforming and social media.

The ancient art of listening.

#22

"To accuse others for one's own misfortune is a sign of want of education. To accuse oneself shows that one's education has begun. To accuse neither oneself nor others shows that one's education is complete." -Epictetus

Epictetus, the Stoic philosopher, taught that personal accountability and understanding of one's control over reactions, rather than events, are very important for personal development.

In the ultimate stage of philosophical maturity, according to Epictetus, we reach a point where we blame neither others nor ourselves for misfortunes. This represents a deep internalization of Stoic principles, where we fully grasp that misfortune typically stems not from events or actions themselves but from our own judgments about them.

Achieving this level of understanding shows complete education, characterized by the acceptance that the only true control lies in our responses and attitudes, not in altering or bemoaning external conditions. A state of profound wisdom and tranquility is the result, free from the turmoil of blame and regret.

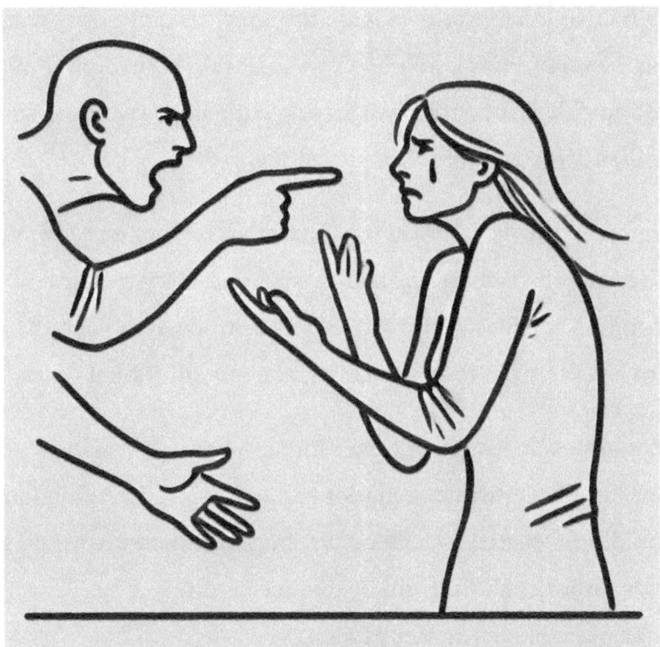

Projecting one's misfortunes upon another.

#23

"Any person capable of angering you becomes your master. He can anger you only when you permit yourself to be disturbed by him." -Epictetus

This quote underlines the idea that emotional responses, such as anger, are within our personal control. By allowing someone to provoke anger, we are essentially giving that person power or control over our emotional state. In modern parlance, we allow that person to "live rent-free in our heads."

Epictetus is focusing here on personal autonomy in emotional regulation. He suggests that we retain power as long as we maintain control over our reactions. When we relinquish that control by reacting with anger, we are giving the other person dominance over our emotional well-being.

We can therefore cultivate a sense of inner peace and detachment from the actions of others, focusing instead on our ability to choose how to respond. This Stoic teaching promotes the idea that true freedom and strength lie in this choice and the refusal to let external circumstances dictate our emotional states.

But what then do we do if someone has caused us truly serious insult, injustice, or injury? Many horrific injurious scenarios come to mind. Certainly, an emotional reaction would be expected in such circumstances. Epictetus would likely argue that action or response should still be divorced from feeling. All action should emerge from a place of reason, not passion.

Social media provides a perfect venue for applying this bit of wisdom. It is the goal of the "troll" to elicit angry responses from those they torment online. In doing so, they feel "mastery" over those people they've attacked. Deny them that satisfaction. By choosing not to be emotionally disturbed, we reclaim both our autonomy and our peace of mind.

Avoid being easily provoked to anger.

#24

"Other people's views and troubles can be contagious. Don't sabotage yourself by unwittingly adopting negative, unproductive attitudes through your associations with others." -Epictetus

This quote advises caution regarding the people with which we choose to surround ourselves and the attitudes we allow into our lives. Epictetus warns that just as diseases can spread from person to person, so too can negative outlooks and unproductive attitudes be transmitted through close associations. He suggests that it's possible to absorb and mimic the negativity and troubles of others, often without conscious awareness.

A quote from motivational speaker Jim Rohn comes to mind: "You are the average of the five people you spend the most time around." Both Epictetus and Rohn remind us that we are often vulnerable to the thoughts, perspectives, biases, and intellectual vulnerabilities of the people with whom we associate most frequently.

To avoid such sabotage, Epictetus seems to be recommending vigilance in our interactions and associations, advocating for a selective engagement that prioritizes our own mental and emotional well-being.

By doing so, we protect ourselves from being swayed by the pessimism and difficulties of others, maintaining a focus on constructive and positive attitudes that foster personal growth and resilience.

The infectiousness of ideas, both good and bad.

#25

"He who laughs at himself never runs out of things to laugh at." -Epictetus

Epictetus was a firm believer in not taking ourselves too seriously. The ability to laugh at oneself is a sign of recognizing one's own imperfections and accepting them as part of the human condition.

This philosophy reflects a deeper Stoic principle of focusing on what we can control and letting go of what we cannot. By accepting and even finding humour in personal shortcomings or misfortunes, we can cultivate resilience and maintain a light-hearted perspective on life's inevitable challenges.

In this way, we can avoid arrogance and continue on our journey of self-improvement and understanding. Laughter becomes not just a response to external situations but a reflective practice that enhances personal growth and emotional health.

It is also a kind of armour. If we can poke fun at our own shortcomings, we become less sensitive about them. This in turn reduces the ability of others to harm us, should they choose to do so by highlighting those same shortcomings.

Laughing at oneself is the finest comedy.

#26

"He is a wise man who does not grieve for the things which he has not, but rejoices for those which he has." -Epictetus

Epictetus conveys a core Stoic principle: contentment and gratitude. Grieving for what one does not have refers to longing, desiring, or feeling sorrow over things that are absent in our lives. According to Stoicism, such feelings are often futile because they concern external circumstances beyond our control.

Rejoicing for what we already have encourages gratitude and appreciation for what is already present and accessible. In this way, we can cultivate a sense of contentment and happiness.

It is useful, as well, to remember that even though we may desire more things, there are those less fortunate who would be very happy to have the things that we take for granted. This refers not just to physical possessions but also to intangible things like relationships.

Wisdom lies in shifting our focus from unattainable desires to the appreciation of our current blessings. This mindset aligns with the Stoic practice of recognizing the limits of our control and finding peace in the acceptance of reality.

Contentment with few posessions.

#27

"First learn the meaning of what you say, and then speak." -Epictetus

With this quote, Epictetus emphasizes the importance of understanding and clarity in communication. He advises that before speaking, one should thoroughly understand the concepts, ideas, or information that one wishes to convey. This requires reflection, study, and comprehension, as speaking without understanding can lead to misunderstandings, errors, and superficial conversations.

Once we have a clear understanding of what we want to express, we can truly communicate effectively. Speaking with knowledge and clarity ensures that the message is conveyed accurately and meaningfully, fostering better communication and understanding.

For example, when speaking to an intimate partner, considering the meaning and intent of our words is important for understanding that the aim is to improve the relationship rather than just to vent frustration. In the workplace, a manager might think carefully before giving feedback, ensuring that the criticism is constructive and clear, helping the employee grow rather than just pointing out faults without guidance for improvement. On social media, we are advised to consider how our words might be misinterpreted by those reading without further context.

Overall, Epictetus advocates for thoughtful and informed speech, stressing the value of being deliberate and knowledgeable in our words to ensure effective and meaningful communication.

Contemplate the meaning of words before speaking them.

#28

"Don't demand that things happen as you wish, but wish that they happen as they do happen, and you will go on well."
-Epictetus

Epictetus teaches that distress arises not from events themselves but from our judgments about those events. By wishing that events occur just as they do, one practices accepting reality without resistance. Stoicism distinguishes between what is in our control and what is not. In line with that teaching, Epictetus is urging us to focus our energy only on the things within our control, mainly our own behaviours, judgments, and reactions. External events, on the other hand, are not up to us; thus, wishing them to be a certain way is both futile and a source of unnecessary distress.

The Latin phrase *amor fati* is often bandied about by Stoics. It means "love your fate", and has some relevance to this quote from Epictetus. Loving ones fate implies accepting the reality of one's circumstance and working to accommodate that reality.

By embracing events as they come, without demanding that they conform to our desires, we cultivate resilience. With resilience, we are better prepared to deal with adversity and unexpected outcomes because we are not tied to a specific expectation of how things should be. This is in contrast to being in a constant struggle with reality, which only leads to unease and distress.

Imagine you are stuck in traffic when you are already late for an appointment. The natural impulse might be to become upset or frustrated. However, by applying Epictetus's advice, you would instead accept the situation as it is, not as you wish it to be. This change in perspective shifts your reaction from frustration to acceptance, reducing stress and helping you to think more clearly about what actions you can take, like notifying those waiting for you of your delay.

In essence, Epictetus is encouraging a shift from desiring control over the uncontrollable to embracing a more serene acceptance of whatever life brings, thereby enhancing one's peace of mind and effectiveness in handling life's challenges.

Accepting one's circumstance with serenity.

#29

"No man is free who is not master of himself." -Epictetus

Epictetus suggests that true freedom is not merely the absence of external constraints but the ability to govern oneself. Being a "master of oneself" involves having control over one's desires, emotions, and reactions. Without this self-mastery, a person is at the mercy of external circumstances and inner impulses, making them effectively enslaved by their own lack of control. True freedom, therefore, comes from within and is achieved through discipline, self-awareness, and the ability to make rational choices independent of external influences.

Furthermore, Epictetus' philosophy aligns with the Stoic belief that inner tranquility and autonomy are paramount. External freedom can be fleeting and is often influenced by factors beyond our control. In contrast, self-mastery provides a stable and enduring form of freedom, as it empowers individuals to maintain their composure, make thoughtful decisions, and live according to their principles regardless of external conditions. By mastering oneself, a person achieves a state of inner freedom that is resilient and unshakeable, reflecting the Stoic ideal of living in harmony with one's true nature and values.

In the realm of personal finance, self-mastery can mean having control over one's spending and saving habits rather than being driven by impulse purchases or consumerist pressures. For those struggling with addiction, the journey towards sobriety is often about gaining mastery over the cravings and compulsive behaviours that once controlled their lives. In a professional setting, mastering oneself can refer to the ability to manage time effectively, prioritize tasks, and remain focused under pressure.

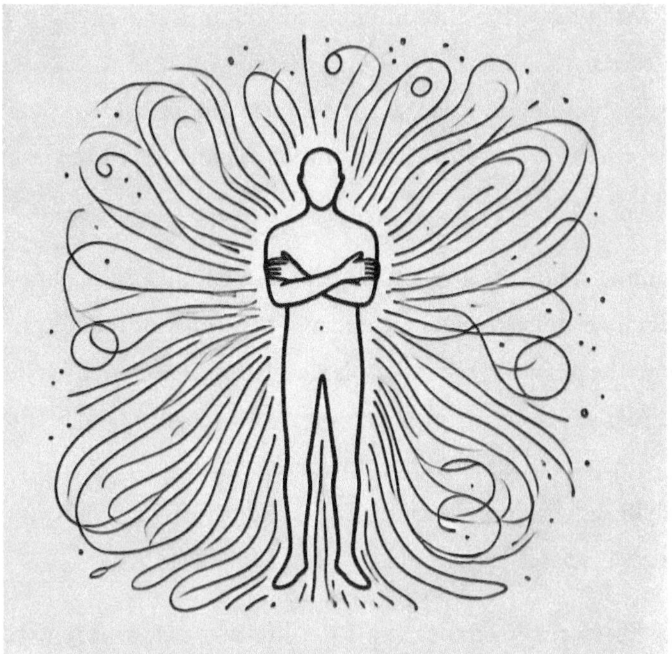

Remain contemplative and resolved in the face of constraints and pressures.

#30

"It is impossible for a man to learn what he thinks he already knows." -Epictetus

Epictetus suggests that when someone believes they already possess complete knowledge on a subject, they close themselves off to new information, insights, and perspectives. This sense of certainty creates a mental barrier that prevents further learning and growth. If a person is convinced that they already know something fully, they are unlikely to seek out additional knowledge or consider alternative viewpoints. This attitude can lead to stagnation and a lack of intellectual development, as it prevents the individual from engaging in the continuous process of questioning, exploring, and expanding their understanding.

This quote underscores the importance of maintaining a mindset of curiosity and humility. True wisdom involves recognizing the limits of one's knowledge and being open to the possibility that there is always more to learn. By acknowledging that our understanding is never complete, we create space for growth and discovery. We must value self-improvement and the pursuit of truth. We should strive to remain teachable, to listen to others, and to be willing to revise our beliefs in light of new evidence or reasoning.

In essence, Epictetus is advocating for a lifelong commitment to learning, grounded in the recognition of our own intellectual limitations.

The stubbornness of certainty.

9 Quotes by Diogenes

D IOGENES WAS GREEK PHILOSOPHER and the most famous adherent to the philosophical school called Cynicism. Perhaps the most entertaining figure of ancient Greek philosophy, he was born in Sinope (in modern-day Turkey) around 412 or 404 BC and died in Corinth in 323 BC. Diogenes is best known for his ascetic lifestyle and his belief that virtue was better revealed in action than in theory.

Cynicism advocates for self-sufficiency, austerity, and shamelessness, often expressed in defiance of social conventions and through simple living. To express his philosophy, Diogenes practiced extreme asceticism, eschewing the physical comforts of a traditional home and instead choosing to live in a large ceramic jar or tub. He owned very few possessions, often only carrying a staff, a bag, and a bowl.

One of the many popular and entertaining stories about Diogenes is that he once saw a child drinking water from his hands. Inspired by this revelation, Diogenes then discarded his bowl, one of his few possessions, stating a person needs no superfluous items.

He is said to have wandered around Athens in broad daylight with a lantern, claiming he was looking for "an honest man," to illustrate the corruption and dishonesty he saw in society. He often expressed his disdain for wealth, power, and respectability, seeing them as irrelevant to the goal of living a proper life.

Diogenes had numerous encounters with other philosophers and figures of his time, perhaps the most famous being with Alexander the Great. According to legend, Alexander found Diogenes enjoying the sun and asked if he could do anything for him. Diogenes replied, "Yes. Stand out of my sun." Such was his disdain for even the most powerful individuals.

Another famous encounter involved fellow philosopher Plato. When Plato asserted that man was "a featherless biped," Diogenes brandished a plucked chicken and shouted, "Behold—a man!"

Perhaps some of these amusing episodes are apocryphal. We cannot know. Regardless, they paint an exquisite picture of a fantastically colourful and eminently quotable character.

Diogenes' commitment to Cynic philosophy had a significant impact on later philosophers, particularly the Stoics, who admired his emphasis on virtue and the ascetic lifestyle.

Diogenes Sitting in His Tub by Jean-Léon Gérôme (1860)

#1

"What I like to drink most is wine that belongs to others."
-Diogenes

Diogenes was endlessly entertaining. This quote highlights his disdain for materialism and personal ownership. As a philosopher of the Cynic school, he advocated for living in virtue and in agreement with nature, eschewing the conventions of society and material excess.

The quote might be a playful remark about enjoying pleasures that come without personal cost or attachment, reflecting his philosophy that true happiness does not come from owning material goods. Or it could be seen as a critique of societal norms and greed. Enjoying something that is not personally owned could be a statement against the accumulation of personal wealth and possessions, which Diogenes saw as unnecessary and burdensome.

Diogenes believed in simplicity and austerity, and perhaps even a communal sharing of resources, challenging the typical values of property and ownership.

The joy of sharing.

#2

"The art of being a slave is to rule one's master." -Diogenes

This remark encapsulates a deeper commentary on power dynamics and personal autonomy.

It is likely that Diogenes is not commenting on literal slavery or dominion, but rather on the influence one can exert over those who seem to be in control. Diogenes suggests that true mastery comes from being able to dictate the terms of our own existence, as well as from our ability to influence those in positions of power, regardless of our social status. This could take the form of managing our reactions, decisions, and integrity in ways that ultimately command respect or dictate the behaviour of those who are nominally "in charge."

From a broader perspective, Diogenes could be seen as advocating for psychological and moral independence. By maintaining our principles and self-control, we might effectively "rule" our masters by not allowing the masters' power to dictate our personal peace or ethical stance. This independence and inner freedom are what Diogenes often preached as true power and liberation.

The quote can be seen as a source of hope for those in positions of subservience. It suggests that if we can maintain a sense of self-worth and inner strength, even in the face of oppression, we may experience a form of psychological empowerment. We might not be able to change our external circumstances much. But we can influence our own responses and reactions. This psychological interpretation of the quote certainly resonates with a Stoic way of thinking.

Regardless of one's station in life, there are ways of maintaining some semblance of autonomy and dignity.

A servant can nevertheless smile.

#3

"Blushing is the colour of virtue." -Diogenes

Blushing, an involuntary and typically genuine reaction, can be seen as a physical manifestation of one's inner moral state or feelings. By associating it with virtue, Diogenes might have been suggesting that true virtue is something that cannot be feigned or concealed. Rather, it is as natural and uncontrollable as blushing. In this way, he contends that genuine virtue is expressed involuntarily, suggesting authenticity and purity.

Blushing is often associated with modesty and humility. When one blushes, it can be seen as a sign of acknowledging one's limitations or mistakes, which are traits often associated with virtuous individuals who embrace humility. An authentic response due to its involuntary nature, blushing suggests honesty, which of course is another core virtue beloved by Diogenes.

Consider a young, relatively new employee who is unexpectedly praised by the senior manager for her exceptional work on a project. The employee, who had worked diligently and without any desire for recognition, begins to blush as her colleagues turn their attention to her. Her state of being visibly moved reflects sincerity and honesty in how she has approached her work. The modern workplace often sees cynicism prevail. But the simple act of expression genuine humility and appreciation at unexpected acknowledgment now uplifts others in the environment, contributing to an improved social dynamic and work culture. Perhaps this is the essence of the type of virtue for which Diogenes is advocating.

The humility and honesty reflected in an involuntary human reaction are a virtue.

#4

"Dogs and philosophers do the greatest good and get the fewest rewards." -Diogenes

Diogenes knows what all dog lovers know, that dogs exhibit purity and honesty. Diogenes would argue that philosophers also strive for both purity and honesty, though often fall short. Dogs, in his view, provide loyalty, protection, and unconditional love without expectation of reward, just as true philosophers offer wisdom and guidance for the betterment of society without seeking personal gain.

Diogenes believed that society often fails to appreciate or reward those who contribute the most to its moral and intellectual welfare. Instead, rewards often go to those who are more interested in personal gain than in genuine contributions to society. Dogs, in their loyalty and selflessness, do not seek material rewards or recognition for their actions. They give freely without expectation of reciprocity or compensation.

This comparison reflects the beliefs of the school of Cynical philosophy, which advocated for a return to a simple, natural way of life, free from pretensions and complications of societal norms. In the eyes of Cynics, both dogs and true philosophers live in accordance with nature and truth, undisturbed by the lack of material rewards or societal recognition.

Diogenes wished that all of us would be driven by intrinsic values and a commitment to the pursuit of wisdom and caring rather than by external recognition or material gain. In essence: to live like a dog. Caregivers, for example, work long hours under stressful conditions, providing critical care, comfort, and support to those under their charge. Their reward is often solely the knowledge that they have contributed.

Both offer valuable yet often unrecognized contributions to society.

#5

"He has the most who is most content with the least." -Diogenes

Diogenes believed that true happiness and fulfillment come from living a life free from unnecessary desires and attachments, finding contentment in what is essential and natural.

Diogenes argues that inner contentment and peace do not depend on external wealth or possessions. Instead, those who can find satisfaction with minimal resources are truly rich because they are not enslaved by material desires or the constant pursuit of more. He valued a minimalist approach to life, in which our needs are reduced to the bare essentials, leading to greater freedom, independence, and happiness.

In essence, Diogenes is advocating for a life of simplicity and self-reliance. He believed that by limiting one's desires and finding contentment with what little one has, a person can achieve a richer, more fulfilling life than one who is constantly seeking to acquire more. This philosophy encourages a focus on inner wealth—such as virtue, wisdom, and self-control—rather than monetary wealth.

The modern application is obvious. Our world is driven by accumulation and consumerism. Today, pursuit of more is often fraudulently seen as a path to happiness. Diogenes reminds us of the emptiness of this promise.

He who has less has more.

#6

"Of what use is a philosopher who doesn't hurt anybody's feelings?" -Diogenes

This quote captures Diogenes's belief that philosophy should be a disruptive force in society, aimed at challenging established norms and provoking thought and self-reflection.

Cynicism, as practiced by Diogenes, advocated for virtue in accordance with a life lived in harmony with nature, free from the influences of societal conventions and materialism. Diogenes used bold, often shocking methods to draw attention to the superficiality he observed in the behaviours of people around him.

Diogenes suggests that a philosopher's duty includes challenging complacency, questioning deeply held beliefs, and pushing others to reflect on their lives and values, even if this process is uncomfortable or painful. In his life, his approach was not to comfort but to stir and awaken, encouraging an exploration of truths that often lie buried under social conventions.

By saying a philosopher should hurt feelings, Diogenes speaks of intellectual and moral rigour that often requires unsettling conversations and encounters, as these are the catalysts for true philosophical inquiry and personal growth.

The quote calls for intellectual courage, and not just for philosophers. It suggests that true inquiry should be fearless in its pursuit of truth and wisdom, even if it means challenging prevailing beliefs or causing discomfort, even to oneself. We should engage with the real world and its complexities, rather than retreating into a comfortable but cowardly position of abstract theorizing or cliched belief systems.

Do not fear discomfort in the quest for truth.

#7

"It takes a wise man to discover a wise man." -Diogenes

Diogenes suggests that that recognizing true wisdom requires one to possess wisdom. Such sagacity is not always easily identifiable by everyone. It requires a certain level of insight, experience, and understanding to discern true wisdom in others. Just as it sometimes takes an artist to fully appreciate another artist's work, or a musician to recognize the skill in another musician, it takes a wise person to perceive and appreciate the qualities of wisdom in another. This is because wisdom involves subtle and profound qualities that may not be apparent to those who lack depth of understanding or experience.

Furthermore, this quote implies that wisdom is a rare and valuable trait, one that can only be fully appreciated and identified by those who have cultivated it within themselves. Perhaps Diogenes is commenting on the reciprocal nature of wisdom: to truly recognize and understand the wisdom in others, one must have a certain level of wisdom. We are thus reminded of the importance of self-cultivation and the pursuit of wisdom in one's own life in order to truly understand and value it in others.

In other words, we must strive for self-reflection, as it is key in identifying resonating traits in others. Consider an organization seeking to hire a new executive. While others have valuable insights and opinions to offer, it is an existing senior executive who is best positioned to identify specific qualities of leadership in candidates.

In a broader sense, the quote It implies that the pursuit of wisdom is not only a personal journey but also a path to recognizing and appreciating wisdom in others.

Now that I have found the best qualities in myself do I recognize them in you!

\#8

"It is not that I am mad, it is only that my head is different from yours." -Diogenes

Oft attributed to Diogenes, on its surface this quote seems to be a defence of eccentric or unconventional behaviours. At a deeper level, it is a call for a society more committed to embracing a diversity of perspectives and thoughts. In many ways, this is a very modern sensibility.

Diogenes suggests that what might be perceived as madness or irrationality by others is actually just a result of having a different way of thinking. His own thoughts and actions are guided by a distinct set of values and principles, which may appear unusual or eccentric to those who adhere to mainstream societal standards. This difference in perspective is not a sign of insanity, he argues, but rather a deliberate choice to question and reject societal norms in pursuit of what he considered a more authentic and virtuous life.

Unconventional or radical viewpoints are often misunderstood and dismissed as madness by those who are entrenched in traditional ways of thinking. In his extreme individuality, he is advocating for intellectual independence and the courage to think differently, even if it means being perceived as mad by others.

The quote hints at the complexity of human cognition. It acknowledges that each individual's mind operates in a unique way, shaped both by their individual biology and experiences, whether personal or cultural. The import of this sentiment resonates loudly in current social conflict, where issues like neurodivergence, diversity, and inclusion are controversial .

The wonderful diversity of human cognition.

#9

"The insult dishonours the one who infers it, not the one who receives it." -Diogenes

Diogenes suggests that when someone insults another person, the act of insulting reveals more about the character and moral integrity of the insulter than of the person being insulted. The person delivering the insult demonstrates their own lack of virtue, respect, and self-control. By resorting to insults, they expose their own pettiness, malice, or insecurity, thus dishonouring themselves.

The person receiving the insult is encouraged to maintain their composure and not be affected by the words of others. If insulted, we are not dishonoured because the insult does not define our worth or character. Instead, our dignity and self-respect remain intact if we choose to rise above the insult and not engage in similar behaviour.

The Cynics, of whom Diogenes was one, maintained a philosophy of valuing inner virtue over external opinions and societal judgments. True honour and integrity are maintained through our own actions and reactions, not through the words or opinions of others.

In the era of social media, the words of Diogenes truly resonate. Imagine a public figure who posts a polite observation on a social media site, only to be mindlessly insulted by anonymous trolls. The public figure is well advised to maintain composure and not reply in kind. We are well advised to remember the modern version of this quote: "Do not wrestle with a pig. You both get dirty and the pig likes it."

Rise above the petty words of those who seek to insult us.

6 Quotes by Xenophon

X ENOPHON WAS AN ANCIENT Greek philosopher, historian, soldier, mercenary, and a disciple of Socrates. He was born around 430 BC in Athens and died in 354 BC. He is most famous for his narration of historical military events, and for his perspectives on moral and military education.

But Xenophon also wrote several Socratic dialogues, the most notable being "Memorabilia," in which he defends Socrates against the charges that led to his execution, presenting a different view of Socrates than the one found in Plato's dialogues.

As a follower of Socrates, Xenophon's philosophical inquiries are practical rather than theoretical, focusing on ethical leadership and effective management of household and state. His works emphasize virtues, such as discipline, loyalty, and justice, and how these can be applied in both military and everyday settings.

Today, Xenophon is commonly studied in military and management schools for his insights on leadership. He believed in practical wisdom and ethical leadership. He advocated for moral integrity and strategic thinking as foundational to successful leadership and societal well-being.

Statue of Xenophon in front of the Austrian parliament in Vienna.

#1

"Self-confidence should always ride side by side with a strong sense of humility." -Xenophon

In this quote, Xenophon is advocating for a balanced approach to self-perception and behaviour. He suggests that while it is important to possess a belief in one's abilities and value, it should be tempered with humility, which involves recognizing one's limitations and the contributions of others.

This balance is important because self-confidence alone can lead to arrogance and overestimation of one's capabilities, potentially resulting in poor decision-making and strained relationships. Humility, on the other hand, helps maintain a realistic assessment of oneself, fosters learning and growth, and enhances interpersonal relations.

Xenophon's insight reflects a deeper wisdom in leadership and personal development. By coupling self-confidence with humility, we can pursue our goals assertively while remaining open to feedback and correction. This approach, he argues, not only leads to personal success but also to a harmonious and cooperative environment.

Confidence and humility.

#2

"People often say what is right and do what is wrong; but nobody can be in the wrong if he is doing what is right."
-Xenophon

The first part of the statement highlights a common human behaviour: expressing knowledge of the right thing to do yet failing to act accordingly. This discrepancy between speech and action is a reflection of human fallibility and moral weakness.

The second part emphasizes that true morality and correctness lie in the actions themselves, not just in speech. If someone's actions are genuinely right, then regardless of previous inconsistencies or the opinions of others, those actions are inherently correct and beyond reproach. This underscores a principle that right actions stand on their own merit.

Someone might profess the importance of kindness and then act selfishly or dismissively towards others. Or a business may claim to support environmental sustainability, but then engages in practices that harm the environment. In an ethical society, actions *should* consistently reflect stated beliefs and values. There is no virtue to be found in merely virtue signalling.

Xenophon, through this statement, stresses the importance of aligning one's actions with one's principles. It serves as a reminder that ethical integrity involves more than just knowing what is right. Rather, it requires the application of these principles in our behaviour. The ultimate measure of our virtue is not what we say but what we *do*.

Walking the walk. Not just talking the talk.

\#3

"Moderation in all things healthful; total abstinence from all things harmful." -Xenophon

Xenophon's guidance serves as a cornerstone of ancient Greek philosophy on living a balanced and measured life. The principle of moderation, or "sophrosyne," is what is being proffered here, distilled to the simple advice that even beneficial habits should not be pursued excessively. Whether it involves physical activities, eating habits, or emotional engagements, moderation is key to ensuring that these beneficial actions do not become counterproductive.

In other words, overindulgence, even in supposedly good things, can lead to harmful outcomes.

Beyond moderation, Xenophon also advises a total avoidance of behaviours or substances that are definitively detrimental to health and well-being. This is a call for a proactive approach to wellness, avoiding known dangers rather than managing their consequences.

In short, a healthy life is achieved by prioritizing harm avoidance and balanced living.

All things in moderation.

\#4

"In the face of danger, be eager, not intimidated." -Xenophon

Xenophon believed that approaching danger with eagerness transforms potential threats into opportunities for demonstrating bravery and therefore for improving character. Eagerness in this case means acting with preparedness, resolve, and a willingness to engage.

This attitude not only helps to grow one's personal fortitude but also inspires confidence in others. It's a blueprint for leadership development in any high-stakes environment, whether it be business, war, or personal conflict.

In Xenophon's view, the best catalyst for personal growth and advancement is headlong confrontation, as opposed to a strategy of self-preservation through conflict avoidance.

If a scary danger is unavoidable, face it headlong.

#5

"No human being will ever know the truth, for even if they happened to say it by chance, they would not know they had done so." -Xenophon

This quote reflects a profound skepticism about human capacity for certain knowledge. It speaks to the limitations in our ability to fully grasp or recognize absolute truth.

Xenophon suggests that truth is elusive and our understanding is inherently limited. Thus, even if one were to accidentally articulate the truth, there would be no sure way to confirm it as such. Xenophon is challenging the confidence with which people often claim to know or express truth, emphasizing the fallibility and uncertainty inherent in human knowledge.

Scientists often use mathematical models to make predictions about complex things like climate change and pandemics. But there are so many uncertainties inherent in these very chaotic systems that it is foolish to make bold and confident statements about the state of those systems, especially in the long term. A proper stance for such scientists, therefore, is humility, open-mindedness, and the readiness to adapt one's understanding in response to new evidence.

Essentially, Xenophon is pointing out that human cognition and perception are not just imperfect but fundamentally incapable of definitively knowing the truth, making our assertions of truth invariably uncertain and tentative. This can be seen as a call for humility in our claims to knowledge and an acknowledgment of the infinite complexity of truth.

Attempting to speak the truth.

#6

"Anything forced is not beautiful." -Xenophon

Xenophon would argue that when something is forced, it lacks the effortless grace and harmony that characterize true beauty. Forced actions or creations often appear contrived, artificial, or insincere, detracting from their appeal and effectiveness. For Xenophon, beauty is intrinsically linked to a sense of naturalness and authenticity, which cannot be achieved through coercion or artificial means.

In broader terms, Xenophon's statement can be applied to various aspects of life. For example, in personal relationships, authentic connections are more beautiful and fulfilling than those that are forced or insincere. In artistic expression, works that flow naturally from the creator's inspiration and skill are more beautiful than those produced under compulsion or artificial constraints.

When an artist tries too hard to impress or follow trends, their work can feel forced and inauthentic. Wearing clothes that don't suit your personal style or make you feel comfortable, but that are nonetheless considered by others to be conventionally attractive, can look awkward or unnatural. A relationship based on pressure or obligation rather than genuine love and affection is unlikely to be fulfilling or long-lasting. A job chosen purely for financial gain or societal expectations may lead to dissatisfaction and a lack of fulfillment.

The beauty of the unforced and natural.

1 Quote by Thales

T HIS VOLUME ENDS WITH a single quote from Thales of Miletus, whom some consider to be the very first philosopher in the Greek tradition. Still others consider him to be among the first true scientists of the Western world. He lived around 624–546 BC and is commonly regarded as one of the so-called "Seven Sages of Greece" (along with six individuals not featured in this book). He is credited with igniting the shift from mythological explanations of the world to more rational inquiries. In this way, he helped to birth the modern world.

Thales is perhaps best known in some circles for his assertion that "water is the principle of all things," positing water as the underlying essence of the material world. By choosing water as this fundamental principle, he sought to explain natural phenomena in a way that was logical and interconnected, moving away from the gods and supernatural explanations that had previously dominated Greek thought.

In science, he is reputed to have predicted the solar eclipse of May 28, 585 BC, which marked a significant moment in the history of astronomy. He is also said to have taught (correctly) that the moon derives its light from the sun, a radical departure from earlier, more supernatural explanations.

In the world of mathematics, Thales is known for having introduced the theoretical and practical use of geometry to Greece. He is said to have been among the first of his era to have calculated the heights of the Great Pyramids, and knew how to compute the distances of ships from shore, all using the theorems of geometry.

In philosophy, Thales is credited with the pioneering view that nature can be explained by natural processes without recourse to supernatural explanations. His lasting influence on both philosophy and science is profound. His teachings marked the beginning of scientific inquiry as we understand it today. So it is proper that his be the final voice in a volume purporting to offer ancient wisdom to a modern world.

Illustration from
"Illustrerad verldshistoria
utgifven av E. Wallis.
volume I": Thales

\#1

"The happy man is the one who has a healthy body, a wealthy soul and a well-educated nature." -Thales

In this quote, we see the three critical pillars that Thales believed were necessary for achieving true happiness and well-being. First comes the physical. According to Thales, a healthy body is foundational, enabling active and full engagement with life's opportunities and challenges. This physical wellness is seen as important not only for personal vitality, but also as a basis for further development in other life areas.

Second comes the spiritual. Beyond physical health, Thales posited that a "wealthy soul," enriched with virtues such as integrity, kindness, and emotional balance, is critical for inner happiness. This wealth is not material but rather a richness of character and spirit, which contributes to a profound sense of fulfillment and peace.

Third comes the mental. A "well-educated nature" encompasses both formal education and a broader, self-directed learning about the world and oneself. Thales believed that intellectual cultivation enhances one's ability to make wise decisions, further contributing to a life well-lived. His holistic approach suggests that true happiness is not singularly focused but is achieved through a harmonious development of body, soul, and mind.

To Thales, the recipe for living a truly fulfilling and meaningful life was straightforward. It must include care for our physical bodies, learning about the world around us, and efforts to be a good and thoughtful person. It's that simple.

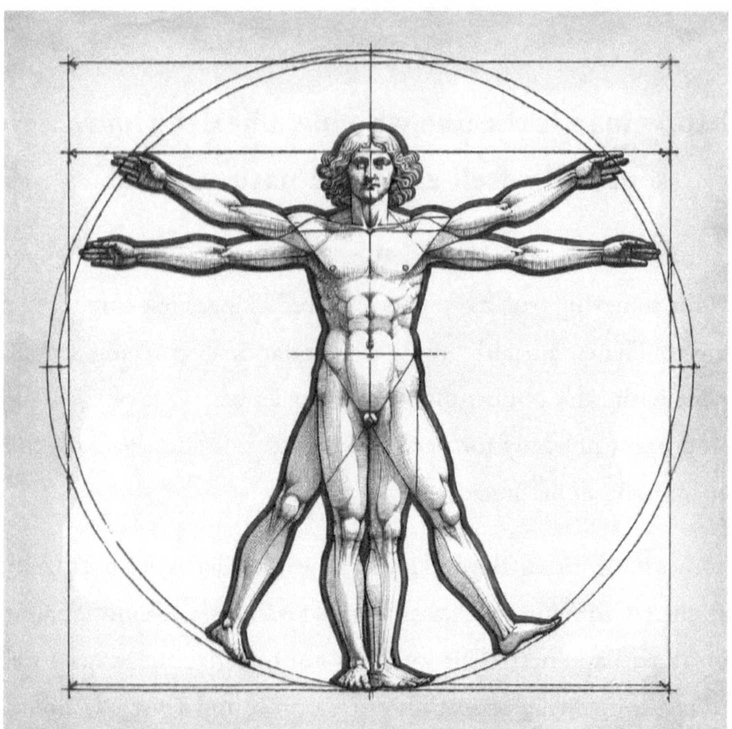

Drawing based on "The Vitruvian Man" by Leonardo DaVinci, representing a well balanced human being.

About the author

Dr Raywat Deonandan is a Professor with the Interdisciplinary School of Health Sciences at the University of Ottawa in Canada. He is a widely published and multiple award-winning writer, as well as a highly decorated educator. In 2000, he was honoured with The Guyana Prize for Best First Work (the national book award of the nation of Guyana) for his debut short story collection, *Sweet Like Saltwater*. In 2016, he was identified by his peers as one of the best teaching professors in the Canadian province of Ontario. As of 2024, he has authored 10 books, and hundreds of newspaper and refereed academic articles. He presently holds a Research Chair in University Teaching.

A Word From the Publisher

We hope you enjoyed this book. If you'd like to keep abreast of upcoming books and be given the opportunity to receive free books, please subscribe to our mailing list at *intanjible.com*.

We promise that we will never send you any spam, and your contact information will never be shared with any outside interests.